SO VEGAN

IN

5

SO VEGAN

IN

5

OVER 100 SUPER SIMPLE
5-INGREDIENT RECIPES

ROXY POPE & BEN POOK

LAGOM
BOOKS FOR A BETTER BALANCED LIFE

'So *Vegan in 5* showcases
fun and simple recipes
and lots of inspiration for
Meat Free Mondays!'

Paul McCartney

'Here is a cookbook that makes it even easier to make delicious vegan food for someone who can't cook at all, like me! Thank you, Roxy & Ben.'

Chris Martin, Coldplay

SO VEGAN IN 5 IS A COOKBOOK FOR EVERYONE, NOT JUST FOR VEGANS.

It's a modern guide to vegan cooking, packed with fuss-free and irresistibly tasty vegan recipes, each using only five ingredients.

We've made it our mission to revolutionise the way we all think about vegan food, proving once and for all that cooking delicious plant-based meals at home can be for everyone (and it's good for the planet, too).

Over the past three years, we've taken our plant-powered message to the masses. Our recipes have reached hundreds of millions of people all over the world and everything we've learned along the way is right here in this book.

We want to debunk the common myths that vegan food is complicated or expensive, so we've made it easier than ever before for people to eat more plants. Whether you're a full-time vegan, a curious carnivore or taking part in a growing movement like Meat Free Monday, let *So Vegan in 5* be your guide to cooking easy, budget-friendly recipes that don't require meat or dairy.

We're talking about go-to recipes you'll want to recreate again and again. Those all-time favourites that never get boring.

We're talking about hearty, home-cooked meals that won't involve spending hours walking up and down supermarket aisles, searching for a never-ending list of ingredients.

We're talking about classic recipes and winning flavour combinations that you can knock together in no time at all, after a long and stressful day at work.

This cookbook is a celebration of vegan food. You'll find over 100 carefully created recipes, including light and wholesome meals, hearty dinners, epic desserts and nutritious nibbles, designed to suit all occasions and developed for the everyday cook.

We've put our hearts and souls into this cookbook, and we really hope you enjoy it as much as we've enjoyed creating it for you.

Roxy and Ben, aka So Vegan

SO VEGAN IN 5

Like most other kids, we never entertained the idea that one day we would actually be vegan.

In both our households, meat and dairy took centre stage on our plates, while the humble plants were pushed to one side. In fact, until only a few years ago, we just assumed vegan food was bland and boring.

At least that was until we tried this vegan thing for ourselves. We decided we wanted to make a difference and we realised that changing our diet would have an immediate and positive impact on the planet, as well as everything that lives on it. And that's when everything changed.

As a result of going vegan, we fell in love with food all over again and we wanted to share this passion with as many people as we could. So Vegan was born shortly after, and ever since then we've been testing, developing and filming recipes for the world to see, all from our cosy flat in South London.

It's unbelievable to think that we now have over a million amazing followers all over the world, and it's difficult to put into words how proud we are to see so many people recreating our recipes at home and sharing our passion for vegan food.

This cookbook is dedicated to everyone who has supported us, believes in our message and is passionate about creating a future powered by plants.

Thanks to everyone who helped to make this possible.

THE 5 THINGS YOU NEED TO KNOW ABOUT THIS COOKBOOK

Before we get going, there are a few important things you'll need to know about *So Vegan in 5* which will help you along the way. Think of these as our top tips for getting the most out of this cookbook.

FINDING YOUR WAY AROUND

You'll notice we've included symbols at the top of every recipe to highlight the prep time, cook time and the cost of making the entire recipe, making it as easy as possible for you to flick through these pages and find exactly what you need. The costs are as follows:

£ up to £3   £ £ £3 - £6   £ £ £ £6+

WINNING COMBINATIONS

We want this cookbook to be your plant-based encyclopedia, so we've covered everything from breakfasts and dinners to snacks and salads. Some of these recipes will provide everything you need for a fulfilling dinner, while you should pair others together for a more nutritious and balanced meal. Keep an eye out for our suggested combinations.

EQUIPMENT

You can't go wrong with a small high-powered blender and a food processor. We've developed a lot of our recipes for two people, which is just how we cook at home, so occasionally you'll need to blend relatively small quantities into sauces and pastes. Trust us, if you can get your hands on a small high-powered blender (or a handheld version) and a food processor, you won't regret it!

ALWAYS CHECK THE LABELS

Occasionally, we'll use ready-made ingredients, such as pastry, sauces and pastes, and sometimes it can be tricky working out which brands are vegan. But don't fret. Always check the labels and remember there's a wealth of information online to help. Most brands will include information on their websites to highlight which of their products are vegan-friendly.

NUTRITIONAL INFORMATION

You'll find all the nutritional info for every single recipe housed neatly at the back of this cookbook. We've also included the following symbols at the top of the recipes to highlight servings that are high in calcium (+240mg), iron (+4mg) and protein (+15g):

THE 5 ESSENTIAL INGREDIENTS

Here are the five must-have ingredients you'll need when working your way around this book. These are the essential extras when it comes to recreating our recipes and you'll see them popping up in various quantities. Be sure to stock up and always have these trusty ingredients on hand:

SALT

We try to avoid using table salt, which is often refined, giving the salt a sharper and less balanced flavour. You'll totally notice the difference using a good-quality sea salt, especially in recipes where we add extra seasoning at the end to bring out all of the flavours. Just be sure to grind the flakes finely to make sure the salt is distributed as evenly as possible.

PEPPER

There's something really satisfying about the punchy aroma of freshly ground black pepper. It makes so much difference compared to the bland pre-ground stuff you'll find in supermarkets. As soon as you grind the peppercorns, all the flavour will begin to escape, and you want as much of that wonderful aroma as possible in your food!

OLIVE OIL

A solid all-rounder when it comes to cooking, 'regular' olive oil has a light complexion because it's usually refined when the oil is extracted. This might remove some of the natural vitamins and flavours, but it also means you're left with an oil that has a higher smoking point, making it less likely to burn when you use it to cook your veggies.

EXTRA VIRGIN OLIVE OIL

This can honestly make the difference between a generic bowl of leaves and a game-changing salad. You want to avoid using this to fry or roast your veggies because the smoking point is a lot lower than regular olive oil. But when it comes to salads or finishing a dish, this golden nectar will add a whole new dimension of flavour to your food.

APPLE CIDER VINEGAR

Super versatile and a core component of vegan cooking, be prepared to see apple cider vinegar popping up all over the place, from our Sun-dried Tomato Pesto (see page 262) to our Mini Passion Fruit Pavlovas (see page 155). The acidity helps balance a lot of our dishes, and it even reacts well with bicarbonate of soda to help cakes rise in the oven.

TAKE THE CHALLENGE: GO VEGAN ONE DAY A WEEK

Maybe you're reading this cookbook as a lifelong vegan. Or maybe you're already a flexi-vegan who is edging closer and closer to living a fully plant-based life. If so, then keep doing what you're doing! We hope our simple five-ingredient recipes will make it easier than ever before for you to enjoy tasty vegan food at home.

Or maybe you're completely new to vegan food. Maybe you want to start making that transition to eating more plants because you know it's one of the best ways to make a positive impact on the planet... but you just don't know where to start.

If that sounds familiar, then we want to challenge you to go vegan one day a week. It's as simple as that. Each week, you pick a day that works for you and you make the commitment to go entirely plant-based.

We know how difficult it can be transitioning from eating meat and dairy every single day of the week to adopting a vegan diet. But if you can start by challenging yourself to go vegan one day a week, then we bet you'll find this transition so much easier.

So Vegan in 5 will help you navigate this new, exciting and modern way of cooking. Our simple, fun and flavoursome five-ingredient recipes will inspire you to rethink your breakfasts, lunches and dinners, so for at least one day a week you can reap the benefits of a plant-based diet.

So are you up for the challenge? Tag #soveganin5 and share your journey!

OCCASIONAL VEGAN

VEGAN 2 DAYS A WEEK

CURIOUS VEGAN

VEGAN 4EVA

VEGAN ONCE IN A BLUE MOON

THE 5 VEGAN MYTHS

We grew up thinking veganism involved sustaining yourself on a diet of raw leaves. But oh how wrong we were. Above all else, veganism is the belief that animals shouldn't be exploited. But beyond that, we've realised it can be whatever you want it to be.

~~Veganism~~

~~is~~

~~extreme~~

1/5

Veganism isn't as black or white as you might think. Some vegans still wear their old leather shoes, while others might choose to avoid buying products that contain palm oil. If you're thinking of going vegan, don't be afraid to go at your own pace. We're all on our own unique journey and remember there's a friendly community ready and waiting if you need advice.

We discover exciting new styles and flavours all the time, which we had no idea even existed before we went vegan! Now we want to show the world how simple it can be to create fun and delicious vegan food at home. There really are endless possibilities when it comes to cooking with plants, so don't be afraid to experiment and create your own twists.

~~Vegan food is boring~~

2/5

Vegans lack important nutrients

3/5

Did you know black beans are packed full with protein? How about the fact that walnuts are a great source of omega-3 fatty acids? Over the past couple of years, we've learned a lot about the food on our plates. You'll need to make sure you're getting enough vitamin B12, but you'll find plenty of healthy plant-based sources for all the other nutrients your body needs.

Some vegetables can be expensive, but so can meat and dairy. The truth is there are ways to be frugal no matter what your diet is, and being vegan is no different. We try to buy quality organic ingredients as often as we can, but occasionally we'll hunt out cheaper alternatives when we're on a tighter budget.

Vegan food is too ~~expensive~~

4/5

Vegan ~~food is~~ ~~complicated~~

5/5

More often than not, cooking vegan food will mean cooking from scratch. This might seem a daunting task and some vegan recipes don't make it easy for you with an endless list of ingredients. But don't panic. We've packed *So Vegan in 5* with over 100 super simple five-ingredient recipes that you'll master in no time.

THE 5 SUSTAINABLE TIPS

Veganism is more than just a diet. It's a lifestyle that involves so much more than the food we choose to put on our plates. The vegan movement has inspired us to do what we can to lower our impact on the planet and contribute to a more sustainable future. Here are our five top tips to do just that:

DO IT YOURSELF

Our bathroom has become a lab for testing homemade deodorants, make up, beauty products and so much more. You'll be surprised by what you can create yourself using natural everyday ingredients. Sugar and beetroot powder double up as a great exfoliant (left: see Ben's beauty regime), and coconut oil is a vital ingredient for a DIY deodorant. You'll find plenty of awesome recipes for natural beauty and skincare products available online.

RE-USE

Nowadays we rarely leave the house without our reusable water bottles and coffee cups. It's become second-nature to carry them with us everywhere we go, and we've now made it a habit to re-use random jars, pots and containers for storing leftovers in the fridge or freezer.

DON'T BE WASTEFUL

Always think twice before throwing leftover ingredients in the bin. Pasta water? That starchy water is full of nutrients, which we feed to our plants. Potato skins? We'll use them to make a stock for soups. And when you think fruit might be going bad, simply chop it up and freeze it in containers, which you can use later for smoothies.

BE PREPARED

This is a lesson we've learned since becoming vegan. Depending on where we're going, it can sometimes be hard to find decent vegan food on the go. So every now and then we'll prep some energy balls, protein bars and smoothies, which means we avoid buying plastic-wrapped food or drinks when we're out and about and in need of an energy boost.

BULK UP

It's so exciting to see more and more people supporting the zero-waste and low-impact movements. We try our best to buy things in bulk as often as we can to cut down on the amount of plastic we use. It's practically impossible to go plastic-free overnight, but there are so many small changes we can all make together that'll have a huge impact.

BREAKFASTS & BRUNCHES

Spiced pear porridge

Harissa tofu scramble

Creamy portobello mushrooms

Smashed peas on toast

Mixed berry chia pudding

Chocolate & hazelnut overnight oats

Peanut butter & jelly breakfast slices

Gingerbread granola

Super-green smoothie bowl

Fluffy blueberry pancakes

Prep 5 mins   **Cook** 8 mins   £   Ca

SPICED PEAR PORRIDGE

This porridge is our ultimate winter warmer and it's ideal for those busy mornings. The comforting blend of cinnamon, nutmeg and ginger in the mixed spice gives this breakfast a lovely fragrant flavour. We'll usually leave the oats and pear to simmer away on the hob while we get ready for the day. So easy.

Makes 1 bowl

1 ripe pear
½ tbsp maple syrup,
    plus extra for serving
½ tsp mixed spice
60g quick-cook oats
250ml soya milk

Peel, halve and core the pear, then cut into 1cm-thick slices.

Place a small saucepan over a medium heat and add the pear slices, maple syrup, mixed spice and 2 tablespoons of cold water to the pan. Cover, bring to the boil, then turn the heat down and simmer for 5–7 minutes.

Meanwhile, prepare the porridge by adding the oats and soya milk to a separate small saucepan. Bring the porridge to the boil, then reduce the heat and simmer for 5 minutes, until the porridge becomes thick and creamy, stirring frequently with a wooden spoon.

Pour the porridge into a bowl, top with the pear mixture and drizzle some extra maple syrup on top. And there you have it, the perfect way to start a winter's day!

Tip
If possible, find pears that are ripe because they'll be extra sweet. Conference pears are available nearly all year round (except in the middle of summer), and they are perfect for this dish.

HARISSA TOFU SCRAMBLE

We use harissa to give this popular vegan breakfast an awesome spicy twist. When it's crumbled, tofu has an uncanny resemblance to scrambled egg and it's even high in protein. We'll always have these ingredients stocked up in our kitchen, so this tofu scramble has become one of our favourite ways to treat friends who pop over for brunch.

Serves 2

1 medium red onion
3 tbsp harissa paste
1 tsp turmeric
280g firm tofu
large handful of rocket

Add a little olive oil to a frying pan over a medium heat. While the oil is heating up, peel and finely slice the onion, then add it to the pan and fry for 5 minutes, stirring frequently.

Meanwhile, combine 3 tablespoons of cold water with the harissa paste, turmeric and a pinch of salt and pepper in a small bowl. Set to one side.

Drain and press the tofu to remove any excess water, then crumble it into the frying pan using your hands. Pour the harissa paste mixture into the pan over the tofu and onion, and stir. Fry for 7 minutes, until most of the moisture has evaporated, stirring frequently with a spoon to break up any big pieces of tofu.

Remove the pan from the heat and serve the scramble, topped with the rocket.

Prep 10 mins   Cook 25 mins   £ £

CREAMY PORTOBELLO MUSHROOMS

Serves 2

60g raw cashews
4 garlic cloves
2 tsp brown rice miso paste
4 portobello mushrooms
small handful of fresh
    flat-leaf parsley

These mushrooms are a total treat. We'll happily gobble these up as they are or serve them as a brunch with our Harissa Tofu Scramble (see page 51).

Preheat the oven to 210°C/190°C fan/gas mark 6.

Transfer the cashews to a small bowl and cover them with hot water from the kettle. Set the bowl to one side and leave to soak until the cashews become soft, about 10 minutes.

Peel and finely chop the garlic, then combine with the miso paste, 1 tablespoon of olive oil and ½ teaspoon of apple cider vinegar in a small bowl to create a paste. Season with a small pinch of salt and pepper.

Clean and trim the mushrooms by slicing 5mm off each stem (the end of the stems can be quite tough), then carefully run a knife around the outside to remove any excess skin that has grown past the gills. Transfer the mushrooms to a baking dish, gills facing up, and use a spoon to cover them with the garlic paste, making sure the mushrooms are evenly coated. Bake in the oven for 25 minutes.

Drain the cashews and transfer them to a small blender along with ½ teaspoon of apple cider vinegar, 100ml of cold water and a pinch of salt and pepper. Blend until smooth.

Serve the mushrooms on a plate and pour the cashew sauce on top. Finally, roughly chop the parsley and sprinkle it over the mushrooms. Heaven.

Tip

We use a handheld electric blender to make the cashew sauce because the quantities are small. If your blender is too big, simply increase the quantities of the cashew sauce and store any leftovers in the fridge – it will keep in a covered jar for up to 5 days.

'We've learned so much about vegan food over the past few years, and everything we know is in this cookbook.'

SMASHED PEAS ON TOAST

Forget about avocados, this is our new favourite way to enjoy a classy bit of toast in the morning. It's healthy, fresh and vibrant, but most importantly, it'll look just as good on Instagram! We're super lucky because our local bakery in Camberwell sells the best sourdough bread in the world (seriously) and it makes the perfect toast for these minty smashed peas.

Serves 2

240g frozen peas
1 garlic clove
½ lemon
handful of fresh mint leaves,
    plus extra to garnish
4 thick slices of sourdough bread

Transfer the peas to a small bowl and cover them with hot water from the kettle. Set to one side for 10 minutes.

Peel the garlic and add the clove to a food processor along with the juice from the lemon, mint, a generous pinch of salt and pepper and ½ tablespoon of extra virgin olive oil.

Drain the peas and transfer them to the food processor, then pulse until the mixture reaches a smooth consistency. You might need to scrape down the sides of the processor as you go to make sure the mixture pulses evenly.

Toast the bread so it's nice and crispy. Spread the pea mixture over the slices of toast, then top with a few more grinds of black pepper and a light drizzle of extra virgin olive oil, and garnish with a few mint leaves. Yum!

MIXED BERRY CHIA PUDDING

We had never heard of chia seeds before we went vegan, but now we use them almost every day because they're a great source of essential nutrients. Chia puddings often look and taste a bit bland, so we've jazzed up this breakfast with a blackberry compote. It turns this breakfast pud an amazing deep-purple colour and it bursts with delicious berry flavours.

Serves 1, generously

125g frozen mixed berries,
    plus extra for decoration
1 tbsp agave syrup
2 tbsp chia seeds
120ml coconut milk (from a carton)
3 tbsp coconut yoghurt

To make the berry compote, transfer the mixed berries and agave syrup to a small saucepan over a medium heat. Simmer for 10 minutes, stirring frequently. We use a wooden spoon to break down the fruit so it reaches a smoothish consistency.

Meanwhile, combine the chia seeds and coconut milk in a small bowl.

Once the berry compote is ready, stir it into the chia mixture, making sure all the ingredients are fully combined. Leave it to cool, then cover and transfer to the fridge for a minimum of 3 hours or overnight.

When you're ready to serve, spoon the coconut yoghurt into a serving glass and use the back of the spoon to smear the yoghurt up the sides of the glass to create a fun pattern. Give the chilled chia mixture a stir, then spoon it into the glass.

Finish with a few frozen berries on top and there you go, our fancy mixed berry chia pudding!

Tip
You can switch this up and use any berries you like, fresh or frozen.

CHOCOLATE & HAZELNUT OVERNIGHT OATS

Serves 1

50g rolled oats
160ml oat milk
1 tbsp cocoa powder
½ tbsp maple syrup
15g whole hazelnuts

Before we decided to go vegan, the idea of eating overnight oats just sounded strange. But now we're totally hooked. Chocolate and hazelnut is just a match made in heaven, while the crunchy roasted nuts perfectly complement the creamy oats.

Combine the oats, oat milk, cocoa powder, maple syrup and a pinch of salt in a container. We use a glass if we're eating the oats at home the next day, or an airtight box if we're eating on the go. Stir to combine, cover the container with a small plate or a lid, then transfer to the fridge and leave overnight.

Before serving the next day, preheat the oven to 200°C/180°C fan/gas mark 6.

Place the hazelnuts on a small baking tray and roast in the oven for 7 minutes or until the hazelnuts darken in colour.

Remove the overnight oats from the fridge and give them a stir. Roughly chop the hazelnuts and stir half of them into the oat mixture, then scatter the rest over the top. Tuck in.

Tips
Prepare the oats in an airtight box if you're in a hurry and then eat them on the go the next day. You can roast the hazelnuts in advance to save time in the morning.

PEANUT BUTTER & JELLY BREAKFAST SLICES

This is the perfect grab-and-go breakfast for anyone who's always in a rush, like us. We'll make these on a Sunday night and they'll last for almost a week in the fridge. You won't believe how much peanut butter the two of us get through, it's our guilty pleasure and we'll add it to everything from smoothies to a coleslaw.

Makes 8 slices

130g crunchy peanut butter
3 tbsp coconut oil
4½ tbsp maple syrup
200g jumbo oats
200g fresh raspberries,
    plus 12 for decoration

Preheat the oven to 220°C/200°C fan/gas mark 7 and line a 450g (approx. 20 x 10cm) loaf tin with baking paper.

Add the peanut butter, coconut oil and 4 tablespoons of the maple syrup to a small pan over a medium heat. Stir until everything has fully combined and the coconut oil has melted.

Meanwhile, transfer the oats to a large mixing bowl. When the peanut butter mixture is ready, pour it over the oats and stir until the oats are completely coated. Add half of the oat mixture to the prepared loaf tin and push down with the back of a spoon to make sure it's compact.

Add the 200g of raspberries and remaining ½ tablespoon of maple syrup to a separate small pan over a medium heat. Simmer for 10 minutes, until it turns into a sauce, stirring occasionally.

When the sauce is ready, spread it evenly on top of the oats in the loaf tin. Top with the remaining oats and use the back of the spoon to press down like you did before. Top with the remaining 12 raspberries. Bake in the oven for 25 minutes or until slightly golden brown.

Remove from the oven and leave to cool for 10 minutes. Use the baking paper to remove the loaf from the tin, and transfer to a wire rack. Leave to cool completely before cutting it into 8 slices. Try not to devour them all in one go!

Tip
It's totally worth investing a little extra in a quality natural peanut butter, which doesn't include added sugar and unwanted additives.

GINGERBREAD GRANOLA

Ben's dad absolutely adores this recipe and he literally hasn't stopped talking about it. It's so easy to make and we love the sweet smells of homemade granola filling our home. You can put your own twists on this recipe by adding anything from cocoa powder and tahini to mulberries and coconut flakes.

Makes 550g

200g mixed dried fruit
       and nuts
270g jumbo oats
130ml maple syrup
1½ tbsp ground ginger
2 tsp ground cinnamon

Preheat the oven to 180°C/160°C fan/gas mark 4 and line a large baking tray with baking paper.

Roughly chop the dried fruit and nuts, then add to a large mixing bowl along with the oats.

In a separate small bowl, combine the maple syrup, ginger, cinnamon, 2 tablespoons of olive oil and a pinch of salt. Pour the maple syrup mixture over the oat mixture and stir until the oats, fruit and nuts are completely coated in the spicy syrup.

Transfer the granola mixture to the lined baking tray and use a spoon to spread it out evenly. Bake in the oven for 20–30 minutes, turning the granola mixture halfway through, so it bakes evenly on both sides.

Remove from the oven and leave the granola to cool before transferring it to an airtight container. We gobble this down in no time, but you can store the granola for up to 1 month.

Tip
We'll always go for a bag with the biggest variety of mixed dried fruit and nuts, containing pistachios, almonds, raisins, sultanas and so much more.

SUPER-GREEN SMOOTHIE BOWL

This is one of our favourite ways to start the day. It's really easy and it's packed with tons of wonderful nutrients. Our homemade Gingerbread Granola (see page 63) is a winner with this smoothie bowl, but you can use a shop-bought version if you're short of time.

Makes 1 bowl

1 ripe banana
½ ripe mango
50g fresh spinach leaves
200ml coconut milk (from a carton)
2 small handfuls of granola

Peel and roughly dice the banana and mango into 2cm pieces, then add the flesh to a freezerproof container and freeze overnight.

The next day, add the frozen banana and mango to a blender along with the spinach and coconut milk. Blend until smooth and combined, then pour into a serving bowl. Top with the granola to serve.

SO VEGAN IN 5

TIP

We're always freezing leftover
fruit so there's something ready
to go when we need to make
a morning smoothie bowl.

Prep 10 mins   **Cook** 10 mins   £   Ca

FLUFFY BLUEBERRY PANCAKES

Serves 2–3

2 ripe bananas
½ tbsp maple syrup, plus
extra for serving
120g self-raising flour
150ml soya milk
90g fresh blueberries, plus
extra for decoration

Roxy is utterly obsessed with pancakes and she's always trying to come up with a new twist on this classic breakfast treat. You can whip these blueberry pancakes up in almost no time at all and they're a satisfyingly indulgent way to start a lazy weekend.

Peel 1 banana and add the flesh to a mixing bowl. Mash with a fork until smooth and no large lumps remain.

Add a pinch of salt, ½ tablespoon of olive oil, the maple syrup, flour and soya milk to the mixing bowl, and whisk until everything is fully combined. Fold in the blueberries.

Heat a little olive oil in a frying pan over a medium-high heat. Once the pan is hot, spoon 2 heaped tablespoons of the pancake mixture into the pan, using the side of the spoon to carefully mould the mixture into a circle, roughly 10cm in diameter. Fry for 2 minutes, then flip the pancake over and fry on the other side for another 2 minutes, until golden brown on both sides. Remove to a plate and keep warm.

Repeat with the rest of the batter, adding a little more oil to the frying pan if the pancakes begin to brown too quickly or start to stick. You should make about 8 pancakes in total.

Peel and slice the remaining banana. Serve the pancakes in a stack with the slices of banana, a sprinkling of extra blueberries and a generous drizzle of maple syrup. Then get stuck in.

Tip
The key to perfecting these pancakes is getting the heat right. Too hot and the pancakes will burn, but if the pan isn't hot enough the pancakes won't cook in the middle.

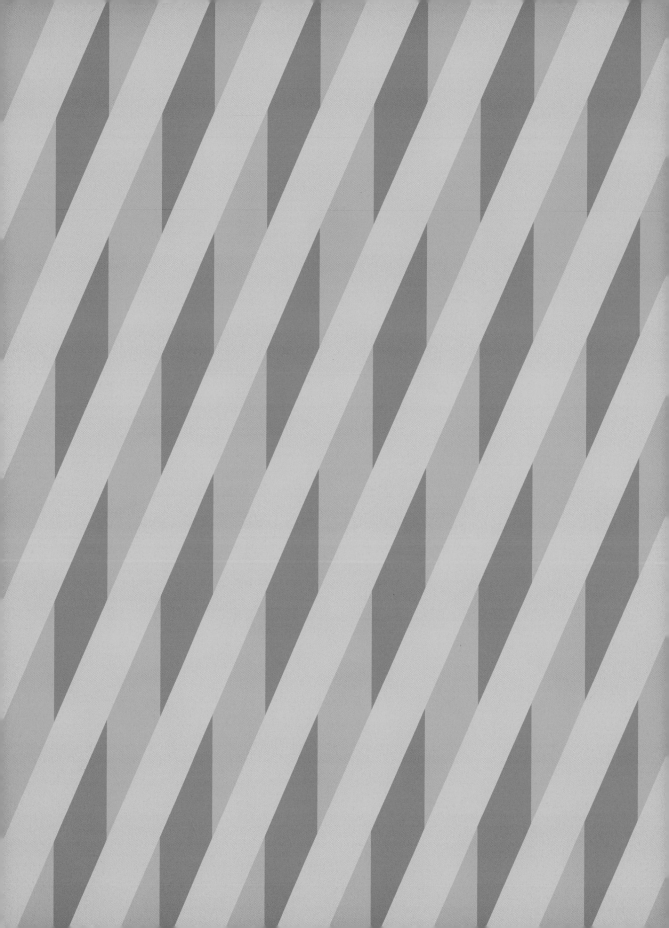

LIGHT MEALS
& SALADS

Fennel, rocket & orange salad

Kale & sweet potato salad

Cajun sweet potato fritters

Thyme & avocado bruschetta

Asparagus tarts

Toasted sesame noodle salad

Roast tomato & basil soup

Roast veg ciabatta sandwich

Tikka tofu skewers

Grilled gem lettuce salad

Mama's beetroot soup

Courgette tempura

Corn chowder

Miso aubergine

Beetroot, apple & coriander salad

Warm Mediterranean couscous salad

Pea & mint soup

FENNEL, ROCKET & ORANGE SALAD

Fennel is a seriously underrated vegetable. We've found ourselves reaching for it over and over again since we decided to go vegan because it's such an easy way to deliver big and bold flavours with minimal fuss. Simply chop it as thinly as you can and throw it together in a salad for a crunchy and refreshing light meal.

Serves 2

1 tsp yellow mustard seeds
1 large fennel bulb
1 red onion
handful of rocket
2 oranges

Heat a small pan over a medium heat. When the pan is hot, add the mustard seeds and toast for 3–5 minutes, stirring regularly, until the seeds are lightly browned and they've started to pop. Set to one side.

Remove the top stalks from the fennel, then slice the bulb in half and chop any hard bits off the bottom. Use a mandoline or a sharp knife to finely slice the fennel and then place it in a large mixing bowl. Peel and thinly slice the red onion, then add to the mixing bowl along with the rocket.

Peel the oranges and cut them into segments over a small bowl to catch the juice, adding the segments to the mixing bowl as you go. We use the membrane of the orange as a guide for where to cut the segments.

To make the dressing, add the toasted mustard seeds, 1 tablespoon of extra virgin olive oil, 1 tablespoon of apple cider vinegar, ½ teaspoon of salt and ½ teaspoon of pepper to the bowl with the orange juice. Mix everything together, then drizzle the dressing over the salad.

Stir to combine, and serve. Job done.

'We're constantly thinking about vegan food, day and night.
We even dream about new recipes in our sleep!'

KALE & SWEET POTATO SALAD

We're obsessed with kale. It's versatile, nutritious and super easy to work with. Lately we've been using this marvellous ingredient raw in salads, mixing it with extra virgin olive oil and massaging the leaves so it becomes lovely and soft.

Serves 2

350g sweet potatoes
120g kale
1 lemon
4 tbsp tahini
1 pomegranate

Preheat the oven to 220°C/200°C fan/gas mark 7.

Rinse and pat dry the sweet potatoes, then cut into 2cm chunks and transfer to a baking tray. Drizzle with a splash of olive oil, season with a pinch of salt and pepper, then combine with your hands. Bake in the oven for 30–40 minutes, until tender.

Meanwhile, rinse and pat dry the kale. Cut out and discard the thick central stalks (see Tip), then slice the leaves into 1cm-thick strips. Add the kale to a large mixing bowl along with a drizzle of extra virgin olive oil and a pinch of salt, then massage it with your hands for 3 minutes to soften the leaves.

To prepare the dressing, squeeze the juice from the lemon into a small bowl, then add the tahini, 4 tablespoons of cold water and a pinch of salt and pepper. Stir to combine, then set to one side.

Cut the pomegranate in half and hold one half over the mixing bowl at a time, seeds facing down, then sharply tap the top with a wooden spoon, until all the seeds fall out into the bowl.

Remove the sweet potato chunks from the oven, then add to the mixing bowl along with the dressing. Give everything a good stir, then serve.

Tip
Save the tough kale stalks to use in smoothies.

CAJUN SWEET POTATO FRITTERS

There's a lot to love about sweet potatoes. They're nutritious and filling, and these fritters will take you less than 25 minutes to make. We'll usually serve these with a simple side salad and our wicked Chipotle Mayo (see page 264).

Serves 2

350g sweet potatoes
2 garlic cloves
2 spring onions
80g plain flour
1 tbsp cajun seasoning

Peel the sweet potato, discarding the skin, then grate the flesh into a mixing bowl. Peel and finely chop the garlic, then trim and thinly slice the spring onions. Add the garlic and spring onion to the bowl along with the flour, cajun seasoning and a pinch of salt.

Combine the mixture using your hands. You'll notice the flour will soak up the moisture from the potato, helping to bind everything together. Split the mixture into 8 parts and shape each eighth into a ball with your hands.

Heat a drizzle of olive oil in a large frying pan over a medium heat. When the oil is hot, add 4 potato balls to the frying pan, and use the back of a spoon to flatten them into the shape of a fritter. Fry for roughly 5-7 minutes, then flip over and fry for a further 5-7 minutes on the other side, until they're lovely and golden brown on both sides. Repeat for the remaining potato balls.

Serve with a sprinkling of extra salt to bring out all the lovely cajun flavours.

Tip
You can also bake these in a moderate oven if you're looking for a slightly healthier option.

THYME & AVOCADO BRUSCHETTA

Serves 2

200g ripe cherry tomatoes
2 fresh thyme sprigs,
    plus extra leaves to garnish
generous splash of
    balsamic vinegar
1 ripe avocado
1 demi (small) baguette

Ben's first true love was Italian food. One of his fondest memories is visiting his local Italian restaurant and ordering their classic bruschetta. Done well using fresh quality ingredients, this simple appetiser can be an absolute joy. Here we switch things up using thyme and avocado for a So Vegan spin.

Halve the cherry tomatoes and add them to a mixing bowl. Pick the leaves from the sprigs of thyme, then add them to the bowl along with the balsamic vinegar, a drizzle of extra virgin olive oil and a pinch of salt and pepper. Stir to combine, then set to one side.

Peel and halve the avocado, remove the stone, then add the flesh to a small mixing bowl along with a drizzle of extra virgin olive oil and a pinch of salt and pepper. Mash with a fork until smooth.

Preheat the grill to high. Prepare the baguette by slicing it in half down the middle, then slice each piece again in half lengthways, leaving you with 4 pieces of baguette. Toast the bread under the grill for a few minutes on each side until golden brown.

Spread some of the mashed avocado onto each piece of toasted baguette, then top with the tomato mix. Serve with a drizzle of extra virgin olive oil and the extra thyme leaves to garnish.

Tip

Did you know that you can use the stone from an avocado to make an exfoliator? Dry out the avocado stone for a few days, then peel and roughly chop it, before adding it to a high-speed blender. You can then use the ground stone as an ingredient in your next natural DIY scrub!

ASPARAGUS TARTS

May to June is officially asparagus season in the UK, during which time these impressive tarts are one of our go-to light meals. We have no qualms using ready-rolled pastry; it makes everything so much easier. You can also use shop-bought vegan pesto, or have a go at making one of our homemade versions (see pages 260–262).

Makes 4 tarts

1 x 320g sheet of
    dairy-free puff pastry
8 tsp vegan-friendly green pesto
12 asparagus spears
200g ripe cherry tomatoes
½ lemon

Preheat the oven to 220°C/200°C fan/gas mark 7 and line a large baking tray with baking paper.

Roll out the pastry so it's approximately 35 x 25cm. Cut it through the middle lengthways and widthways to create 4 rectangular tarts, then transfer them to the lined baking tray.

Spread 2 teaspoons of pesto onto each tart, leaving roughly 2cm clear around the edges.

Trim the asparagus spears so that they fit into the tarts, discarding the ends. Add the asparagus to a mixing bowl along with a drizzle of olive oil and a pinch of salt and pepper. Halve the cherry tomatoes, add them to the mixing bowl and stir everything to combine.

Place 3 asparagus spears onto each tart, followed by a few tomato halves.

Brush the edges of the tarts with olive oil, then bake in the oven for 18–20 minutes, until the pastry is cooked and golden brown.

Remove the tarts from the oven. Top each with a squeeze of juice from the lemon and a few extra grinds of pepper, then serve.

TOASTED SESAME NOODLE SALAD

This noodle salad is all about the toasted sesame seeds. They have an intense nutty flavour and bring a wonderful crunch to the dish. You can easily prepare this one evening and leave it in the fridge overnight for a nutritious and light lunchtime meal the next day.

Serves 2

4 tbsp sesame seeds
120g dried soba noodles
    (or wholewheat noodles)
2 tsp tamari (or soy sauce)
2 medium carrots
large handful of fresh coriander

Add the sesame seeds to a dry frying pan set over a medium-high heat and cook for 5–7 minutes, until they turn brown. Keep a close eye on the pan and shake it regularly to prevent the seeds from burning.

Meanwhile, cook the noodles as per the packet instructions, which usually involves cooking them in a pan of boiling salted water for 5 minutes. As soon as the noodles are ready, drain and rinse them under cold water to stop any further cooking. Transfer the noodles to a large mixing bowl.

Once the sesame seeds are toasted, transfer them to a pestle and mortar, but leave ½ tablespoon or so to one side to use for topping. Grind the seeds until they reach a flour-like texture, which will take a few minutes and lots of elbow grease!

Add the tamari to the ground seeds along with 2 tablespoons of extra virgin olive oil, ½ teaspoon of apple cider vinegar and a generous pinch of pepper, then mix everything together into a paste. Transfer the sesame paste to the bowl with the noodles.

Next, use a veggie peeler to peel the carrots into long strips, then add these to the noodles. Roughly chop the coriander and add most of it to the noodles, leaving some to one side for topping.

Mix the ingredients together in the bowl until the delicious sesame paste has coated everything, then divide the noodles into 2 serving bowls. Top with the remaining coriander and toasted sesame seeds, then serve.

SO VEGAN IN 5

ROAST TOMATO & BASIL SOUP

Tomato soup is possibly the greatest soup of all time. Growing up, a bowl of tinned tomato soup felt like a heavenly treat and a remedy for those poorly days spent at home. These days, however, nothing beats one that's freshly made at home. Our version comes with all that healthy stuff and it's packed with the fresh flavours we love.

Serves 2

800g ripe tomatoes
3 garlic cloves (skin on)
1 onion
small handful of fresh basil,
    plus extra to garnish
350ml vegetable stock

Preheat the oven to 200ºC/180ºC fan/gas mark 6.

Fill a large bowl with boiling water straight from the kettle. Score a little cross into the top of each tomato to make them easier to peel later on, then add the tomatoes to the bowl, making sure they are totally submerged in the water. Leave the tomatoes to soak for 1 minute, before removing them and leaving to cool for a couple of minutes. Once the tomatoes are cool enough to handle, peel away and discard the skins.

Slice the tomatoes into quarters and transfer them to a baking tray. Season them with a generous pinch of salt and pepper and a drizzle of olive oil, using your hands to rub in the seasoning. Bake in the oven for 30 minutes.

Remove from the oven and add the whole garlic cloves to the tray. Bake for a further 10 minutes.

Meanwhile, add a little olive oil to a frying pan over a medium heat. Peel and slice the onion, then add it to the pan and fry for 10 minutes or until caramelised, stirring frequently.

Transfer the onion to a blender along with the stock and the leaves from the basil. Remove the baking tray from the oven and transfer the tomatoes with all their juices to the blender. Once the garlic is cool enough to handle, peel it and add the flesh to the blender. Blend until smooth.

Transfer the soup to a saucepan and bring to the boil, then reduce the heat and simmer for 10 minutes. Taste the soup and season with salt and pepper, as desired.

To serve, divide the soup between 2 bowls, drizzle with extra virgin olive oil, top with a few grinds of black pepper and garnish each portion with a basil leaf.

Tip
Every now and then we'll make a big batch, leave it to cool, then freeze it for a rainy day.

ROAST VEG CIABATTA SANDWICH

Roxy spent a few years working in Hampstead where her favourite local deli served the finest roast veggie sandwich. It fast became her staple midday meal, so it felt only right to recreate our own version for this cookbook. Have a go at making your own hummus using one of our recipes (see pages 225, 234–235).

Serves 2

1 courgette
2 peppers (mixed colours)
2 ciabatta rolls
1 tbsp vegan-friendly green pesto
2 heaped tbsp hummus

Preheat the oven to 200°C/180°C fan/gas mark 6 and line a large baking tray with baking paper.

Trim the ends off the courgette and cut it in half, then cut each half into 5mm-thick strips. Halve the peppers and remove the seeds, then slice into 2cm-thick strips. Transfer the veg to the lined baking tray and sprinkle with a pinch of salt and pepper, then drizzle with olive oil. Combine everything with your hands, spread the veg out in an even layer, then bake in the oven for 20 minutes or until soft.

Cut the ciabatta rolls in half, add them to the oven and bake everything together for a further 5 minutes.

Remove the ciabatta and veggies from the oven and spread ½ tablespoon of pesto on the bottom half of each roll. Then add a generous layer of courgette and pepper strips.

Spread a heaped tablespoon of hummus inside the remaining half of each ciabatta roll and place them on top. Tuck in and enjoy.

Prep 15 mins, plus 2 hours marinating   **Cook** 16–20 mins   £ £   Pr Ir

TIKKA TOFU SKEWERS

We usually prep these skewers the day before and leave them to marinate in the fridge overnight. But be warned... they never last long at our BBQs, even among the meat eaters, so keep a close eye on them if you want one for yourself!

Serves 2

300g extra-firm tofu
2 peppers (mixed colours)
2 tbsp tikka masala paste
3 tbsp soya yoghurt
1 lime

Press the tofu to remove any excess water, then slice it into 12 even pieces. Halve the peppers and remove the seeds, then cut into squares the same width as the tofu to ensure everything cooks evenly.

Mix the tikka masala paste with the soya yoghurt in a large mixing bowl. Add the tofu and peppers to the tikka marinade, and mix everything together carefully using your hands. Cover and leave to marinate in the fridge for at least 2 hours.

When you are ready to cook, thread a slice of pepper onto a metal skewer (or see Tip) followed by a piece of tofu. Repeat until there are 3 pieces of tofu on the skewer and roughly 4 slices of pepper. Repeat for the remaining 3 skewers.

Heat a little olive oil in a griddle pan over a medium-high heat. Once hot, add the skewers and fry for 8–10 minutes on each side or until the tofu starts to char, which will add to the flavour!

Remove the skewers from the griddle pan and serve on a plate with a squeeze of lime juice and a pinch of salt.

Tip
If you are using wooden skewers, be sure to soak them in water for 30 minutes before use – this prevents them from burning during cooking.

GRILLED GEM LETTUCE SALAD

Serves 2

180g radishes
2 Little Gem lettuces
2 tbsp tahini
1 lemon
400g tin butter beans

We'll knock together this warm and colourful salad when we're craving something light, fresh and a little bit fancy! Just don't be shy with the rich tahini and lemon dressing, which pulls together the entire dish.

Preheat the oven to 200°C/180°C fan/gas mark 6.

Trim the ends off the radishes, slice them in half and place on a baking tray. Drizzle with a little olive oil and bake in the oven for 15 minutes or until soft at the edges.

Meanwhile, pour a little olive oil into a griddle pan set over a medium heat. Halve the lettuces, rinse them under cold water and pat dry. Season both sides of the lettuce halves with a pinch of salt and pepper, then place on the hot griddle pan and cook for 3 minutes on each side.

In the meantime, prepare the tahini dressing by combining the tahini with the juice from half of the lemon and 3 tablespoons of cold water in a small bowl. Stir until you have a smooth and runny dressing. You may have to add a little more water if your tahini is thick. Set aside.

Drain and rinse the butter beans, then add half to a separate small bowl. Mash them with a fork, then add the remaining beans along with a pinch of salt and pepper and a drizzle of extra virgin olive oil. Stir to combine.

To serve, place 2 grilled lettuce halves on a serving plate, crumble half of the butter bean mixture on top and garnish with half of the baked radishes. Repeat for the second plate.

Drizzle over the tahini dressing, followed by a splash of extra virgin olive oil, then drizzle over the juice from the remaining half of the lemon. Top with a little lemon zest to finish.

Tip
We combine leftover lemon peel with white vinegar to create a homemade all-purpose cleaner.

MAMA'S BEETROOT SOUP

Growing up with a Polish mum, Roxy was no stranger to the likes of *pierogi* (dumplings) and *bigos* (stew). But what stands out more than anything else is *barszcz*, aka beetroot soup. And nobody does this classic Polish dish better than Roxy's mum, obviously.

Serves 3–4

500g raw beetroot
1 litre vegetable stock
400g potatoes
small handful of fresh dill,
    plus extra to garnish
1 lemon

Trim off and discard the ends of the beetroot and peel. Cut the beetroot into 1cm-thick slices and add to a large saucepan along with the vegetable stock. Bring the soup to the boil, then reduce the heat and simmer for 10 minutes.

Meanwhile, peel the potatoes and slice into 2cm chunks.

Add the potato chunks to the saucepan and bring the soup to the boil again, then reduce the heat and simmer for 15 minutes, until the veg are tender, stirring occasionally.

Remove from the heat, pour the soup into a blender (or carefully use a handheld blender in the pan), then add the dill and juice from the lemon. Blend the soup until smooth, then taste and season with salt and pepper.

To serve, ladle the soup into bowls, then top each serving with a drizzle of extra virgin olive oil and a sprinkling of chopped dill.

COURGETTE TEMPURA

This tempura is easier than you might think and you'll be left with something that's light, crispy and fun to share around the dinner table. Don't fuss over making things look pretty, we'll usually throw these together on a tray alongside a pot of sweet chilli sauce. Job done.

Serves 4

2 large courgettes
1 litre vegetable oil
150g self-raising flour
1 tbsp cornflour
80ml sweet chilli sauce

Pour 300ml of cold water into a freezerproof container and leave it in the freezer for 10 minutes.

Cut the courgettes into 5mm-thick diagonal slices and set aside.

Pour the vegetable oil into a small deep-sided frying pan on a medium–high heat, ensuring the oil is 5cm deep in the pan. Leave the oil on the heat while you prepare the batter.

Add the self-raising flour, cornflour, ½ teaspoon of salt and ½ teaspoon of pepper to a mixing bowl, and stir everything together with a whisk. When the water in the freezer is ice-cold, add it to the mixing bowl and whisk all the ingredients together to form a batter. Check the oil is hot enough by dropping in a little batter. The batter will sizzle and brown within 60 seconds when the oil is ready.

Dip the courgette pieces into the batter one by one, gently shaking off any excess batter as you go. Then carefully drop the courgette pieces into the hot oil one by one (always drop them away from you). We usually fry in batches of 4 or 5 pieces at a time so the pan doesn't get overcrowded. Fry for 1 minute, then turn the courgette pieces over and fry for a further minute until the batter is light and crispy.

Remove the courgette pieces from the frying pan and place them on a few sheets of kitchen towel to absorb any excess oil.

Repeat until all of the courgette pieces have been used up.

Serve the Courgette Tempura with a side of sweet chilli dipping sauce, or have a go at making our delicious Chipotle Mayo recipe on page 264. You won't regret it!

Tip
Be really careful as the oil will get very hot. If the oil starts to bubble, simply reduce the heat.

CORN CHOWDER

This is the perfect remedy when the weather has forced you indoors. We use a touch of soya cream to thicken the soup, but a lot of that traditionally creamy texture comes from blending half of the chowder and simply adding it back in with the rest. It's optional, but well worth the minimal fuss.

Serves 2

3 garlic cloves
200g potatoes
60ml soya cream,
    plus extra for serving
500ml vegetable stock
230g frozen sweetcorn

Heat a little olive oil in a saucepan on a medium heat. While the oil is heating up, peel and dice the garlic, then add it to the saucepan and fry for 2 minutes, stirring frequently to make sure it doesn't burn.

Peel and cut the potatoes into 2cm chunks. Add them to the saucepan along with the soya cream, vegetable stock, 1 teaspoon of apple cider vinegar and 200g of the sweetcorn. Bring the soup to the boil, then reduce the heat and simmer with the lid on for 15-20 minutes or until the potatoes are soft.

Meanwhile add the remaining sweetcorn to a frying pan on a medium-high heat and fry for 5 minutes, stirring frequently until it has turned golden brown. Set the sweetcorn to one side while the soup finishes cooking.

Transfer half of the soup to a blender and blend until smooth, then stir it back into the saucepan with the remaining soup. Taste and season to your liking with salt and pepper.

Serve the soup with a drizzle of soya cream, half of the fried sweetcorn per serving and freshly ground black pepper.

MISO AUBERGINE

There is something undeniably satisfying about the combination of miso and aubergine. We add some fresh chilli for heat, agave for sweetness and cucumber for a refreshing finish.

Serves 2

2 aubergines
3 tbsp brown rice miso paste
1 tbsp agave syrup, plus extra
160g cucumber
1 fresh red chilli

Preheat the oven to 200°C/180°C fan/gas mark 6.

Slice the aubergines in half lengthways and place them skin-side down in an ovenproof dish. Then use a knife to score a diagonal pattern in each half.

Combine the miso paste, agave syrup, 1 tablespoon of olive oil and a generous pinch of pepper in a small bowl. Spread the mixture evenly over the scored aubergine halves. Cover the dish with a lid or with foil, then transfer to the oven for 25 minutes.

Meanwhile, use a peeler to cut the cucumber into thin strips and add to a small bowl. Discard any excess water, then season the cucumber with a pinch of salt and pepper, and 1 teaspoon of apple cider vinegar. Mix everything together, then leave the bowl to one side.

Take the aubergine out from the oven, remove the lid or discard the foil and place the ovenproof dish back in the oven for a further 20-25 minutes, so the tops of the aubergines become crispy while the insides are soft and juicy.

Remove the aubergines from the oven and leave them to one side while you prepare the toppings. Slice the chilli into rings, removing any seeds as you go if you don't like your food too hot. Drain the cucumber again to remove any excess water, then mix in a small squeeze of agave syrup.

To serve, top the aubergine halves with the red chilli slices and cucumber strips.

Tip
The miso we use is already very salty, so we don't add extra salt to the aubergine. But trust your own palate and do what you think is best.

BEETROOT, APPLE & CORIANDER SALAD

Serves 4

3 medium raw beetroots
1 garlic clove
2 Granny Smith apples
70g radishes
large handful of fresh coriander,
    plus extra for serving

This vibrant salad is bursting with colour. It's fresh, full of flavour and it's now our go-to recipe when we have friends visiting and we want to prepare a healthy and nutritious meal. Usually we'll cook the beetroot in advance and simply prepare the salad when it's needed. Easy.

Preheat the oven to 220ºC/200ºC fan/gas mark 7.

Wrap the beetroots in a piece of foil and cook them in the oven for 45 minutes – 1 hour depending on the size of your beetroot. When the beetroots have finished cooking, discard the foil and leave them to cool while you prepare the rest of the salad.

To make the salad dressing, peel and finely chop the garlic, then combine it with 2 tablespoons of extra virgin olive oil, 2 tablespoons of apple cider vinegar and a generous pinch of salt and pepper in a small mixing bowl, then set aside.

Remove the cores from the apples and slice them into 16 wedges. Trim the ends off the radishes and thinly slice them using a sharp knife or a mandoline. Roughly chop the coriander and add it to a large salad bowl along with the apple wedges and slices of radish.

Once the beetroots are cool enough to touch, peel and discard the skins, then cut them into eighths and add the beetroot wedges to the salad bowl.

Pour the salad dressing into the salad bowl and stir to combine.

Serve with a sprinkling of extra chopped coriander.

Tip
We love Granny Smith apples because they're crunchy and tart, but you can substitute these for Cox or even Golden Delicious if you prefer.

WARM MEDITERRANEAN COUSCOUS SALAD

Serves 2

300g ripe cherry tomatoes
120g giant couscous
50g mixed fresh olives, pitted
handful of fresh basil
150g cucumber

This is a wonderfully warm and colourful summer meal. Giant couscous is a joy to cook with; it's filling and slightly chewy, and here it teams up superbly with the comforting classic flavours of the Mediterranean.

Preheat the oven to 200°C/180°C fan/gas mark 6.

Halve the cherry tomatoes and add to a baking tray. Drizzle with a light splash of olive oil and season with a generous pinch of pepper. Shake the tomatoes around the tray to make sure they're evenly coated, then bake in the oven for 20 minutes or until they start to collapse.

Meanwhile, add the couscous to a small saucepan along with 300ml of cold water. Bring to the boil, then reduce the heat to a simmer and cook the couscous with the lid on for 10 minutes. The couscous will be ready when it's soft but still slightly chewy.

Slice the olives in half and finely chop the basil, then place both in a mixing bowl. When the couscous has finished cooking, drain it and add to the bowl.

Check the tomatoes. If they are ready, remove from the oven and gently mash half of them with a fork to release the juices, then transfer all of the tomatoes and their juices to the mixing bowl.

Dice the cucumber and add it to the bowl along with 1 tablespoon of extra virgin olive oil and 2 teaspoons of apple cider vinegar, then stir everything together to combine all the amazing flavours.

Taste and season with salt and pepper, then serve.

TIP

We'll often try to find good-quality olives which have already been marinated in herbs. This is a clever way to introduce even more flavour to this awesome salad.

PEA & MINT SOUP

Pea and mint is one of our favourite flavour combinations. This soup is light, fresh and colourful, and it's so simple to make you'll have it mastered in one go.

Serves 2

5 spring onions
500ml vegetable stock
450g frozen peas
5 fresh mint sprigs,
    plus extra to garnish
½ lemon

Trim the ends off the spring onions and roughly chop into thin slices. Add a little olive oil to a saucepan over a medium heat. Once hot, add 4 of the chopped spring onions and fry for 5 minutes, until tender, stirring frequently.

Add the stock and peas to the pan, and bring the soup to the boil, then reduce the heat and simmer for 4 minutes.

Pick the mint leaves off the stalks and add the leaves to a blender, along with the soup and juice from half the lemon, then blend until smooth. Taste and season with salt and pepper. Note: you may need to add a large pinch of salt, depending on how salty your vegetable stock is!

To serve, pour into bowls, drizzle with extra virgin olive oil, top with the remaining chopped spring onion and garnish with a few mint leaves.

DINNERS

Rich ragu

Black bean mushrooms on noodles

Hoisin jackfruit bao buns

Spicy gnocchi

Broccoli Alfredo

Butternut squash naan breads

Deep-pan pizza

Creamy spinach ravioli

Whole-roasted cauliflower korma

Mushroom, sage & onion wellington

Super squash tray bake

Peanut butter tofu zoodles

Loaded sweet potatoes

Artichoke & tapenade pasta

Minced mushroom tacos

Apricot & rosemary nut roast

Pulled bbq mushroom burgers

Spinach & tofu filo pie

Purple linguine

Ratatouille swirl

Za'atar cauliflower steaks

The carnival tofu burger

RICH RAGU

There's a lot to love about this ragu pasta; the intensity of the flavour, the simplicity of it, the fact that you have the perfect excuse to enjoy it with the bottle of wine you just cracked open. We find ourselves returning to this dish again and again. Maybe it's the fact that this reminds us of eating homemade spag bol as kids. Except this is way better.

Serves 2

4 frozen vegan sausages
200g pappardelle (or tagliatelle)
100ml vegan-friendly red wine
400g tin plum tomatoes
1 tbsp brown rice miso paste

Defrost the sausages in a microwave or leave them out at room temperature for a few hours to defrost. Once defrosted, mash them up in a bowl using a fork.

Add the minced sausages to a pan over a medium heat and fry for 10 minutes, until the sausage mixture starts to crisp, stirring occasionally. The sausages shouldn't require any additional oil, but depending on what brand you use, you might want to add a small splash of olive oil to prevent any sticking to the pan.

Meanwhile, cook the pasta in a pan of boiling salted water as per the packet instructions.

Add the red wine to the sausage mixture and cook it for a couple of minutes so the alcohol evaporates. Add the tinned tomatoes and miso paste and stir everything together. Leave the delicious ragu to simmer gently for 10 minutes, stirring occasionally.

Season the sauce with a very generous pinch (or two) of pepper. It shouldn't require any additional salt because the miso paste is already quite salty. Give it a final stir, gently breaking down any remaining tomatoes with the back of a wooden spoon.

Drain the pasta and combine it with the ragu sauce, then serve with a light splash of extra virgin olive oil. Simple and delicious.

Tip

Lots of supermarkets sell vegan wine, but they don't always say it's vegan. You'll find plenty of resources online, like barnivore.com, to help you identify which brands are vegan-friendly.

BLACK BEAN MUSHROOMS ON NOODLES

Serves 2

½ thumb-sized piece of fresh ginger
1½ tbsp black bean garlic sauce
4 portobello mushrooms
120g dried soba noodles
    (or wholewheat noodles)
150g cucumber

It's becoming a lot easier to find authentic ready-made sauces on the high street. Black bean garlic sauce is without doubt one of our favourites. It has an intense earthy flavour and pairs perfectly with portobello mushrooms.

Preheat the oven to 200°C/180°C fan/gas mark 6.

Peel and finely dice the ginger. Add it to a small bowl along with the black bean garlic sauce, 1 tablespoon of olive oil and 2 tablespoons of cold water, and mix everything together to make a sauce.

Clean and trim the mushrooms by slicing 5mm off the tough stems, then carefully run a knife around the outside to remove any excess skin that has grown past the gills.

Place the mushrooms in an ovenproof dish, pour the sauce on top and and then use a pair of tongs to mix everything together so the mushrooms are fully coated in the sauce. Make sure the mushrooms are sitting with their gills facing up and most of the sauce is on top of the mushrooms, then cover the dish with a lid or foil and cook in the oven for 30 minutes, until tender.

Ten minutes before the mushrooms are ready, add the soba noodles to a saucepan of boiling salted water. Bring to the boil and cook as per the packet instructions (usually 5 minutes), then drain.

Remove the mushrooms from the dish and gently shake off any excess sauce back into the dish. Dice the cucumber into small pieces and add three-quarters to the dish, along with the noodles. Mix everything together, making sure the noodles are coated in the delicious sauce, then season to taste (the sauce is already quite salty, so we simply add a pinch of pepper).

Divide the noodle and cucumber mixture between 2 plates, place 2 mushrooms on top of each portion, then scatter over the remaining diced cucumber. If there's any leftover sauce in the dish, drizzle it on top, then serve.

HOISIN JACKFRUIT BAO BUNS

These awesome buns are always a crowd-pleaser. We're big fans of making food we can eat with our hands; it's fun, messy and there's usually less washing up at the end!

Makes 8 small buns

250g self-raising flour,
    plus extra for dusting
200ml coconut milk (from a carton)
550g tin jackfruit in water
2 tbsp hoisin sauce,
    plus extra for serving
½ large cucumber

Sift the flour into a bowl, then add the coconut milk and a generous pinch of salt, and mix everything together.

Transfer the dough to a floured work surface and use your hands to roll it out into a long log, adding pinches of flour as you go if it's too sticky. Divide the dough into 8 even-sized pieces. Roll each piece between your hands for 15–20 seconds, working to remove any creases in the dough, then use a floured rolling pin to roll each piece of dough into a circle roughly 8cm in diameter.

Line the trays of a steaming basket with baking paper and poke holes in the paper to allow the steam to come through. Lightly brush the top of each circle of dough with olive oil, fold each circle in half and transfer to the steaming basket. Leave a 2cm space between each bun so they don't touch, because they'll grow in size as they steam.

Cover the basket with a lid, then place it on top of a saucepan of boiling water and steam the buns for 10–12 minutes. Check after 10 minutes – the dough should have doubled in size. If it's still moist in the middle, then leave it to steam for another couple of minutes.

Meanwhile, drain and rinse the jackfruit in cold water. Slice off the tough triangular pieces (the core), cut them into thin slices and set aside. Add the remaining jackfruit to a bowl and use a fork to shred it apart.

Add all the jackfruit to a frying pan and fry over a low-medium heat for 7 minutes, stirring occasionally. Add the hoisin sauce and ½ teaspoon of apple cider vinegar and season well with salt and pepper. Cook for a further 3 minutes.

Meanwhile, use a veggie peeler to cut the cucumber lengthways into long thin strips (discarding the seedy centre).

To serve, fill each bun with a heaped tablespoon of the jackfruit mixture, a couple of cucumber strips and a generous drizzle of extra hoisin sauce.

Tip
We buy tinned jackfruit from our local Asian supermarket, but we've also noticed it in some big supermarkets.

SPICY GNOCCHI

We love to tuck in to this spicy gnocchi when it's cold outside and we're snuggled up on the sofa watching TV. This is simple cooking at its best.

Serves 2

small handful of fresh basil,
    plus extra for serving
400g tin plum tomatoes
2 tbsp chilli garlic sauce
380g potatoes
110g plain flour,
    plus extra for dusting

Roughly chop the basil and add it to a frying pan along with the tinned tomatoes, chilli garlic sauce and 2 teaspoons of apple cider vinegar. Simmer gently for 20 minutes, stirring occasionally, then keep warm over a low heat.

Meanwhile, peel the potatoes and cut into 3cm chunks, then add to a pan of boiling salted water for roughly 12–14 minutes or until completely soft.

Remove the potatoes from the saucepan and transfer to a mixing bowl, reserving the starchy water to cook with later. Leave to steam for a few minutes so the moisture escapes, then mash the potatoes until completely smooth. Season generously with salt and pepper, then transfer the mash to a large floured surface.

Add the flour to the mashed potato in stages, using your hands to mix everything together. Gently fold the dough a few times until the mash and flour are fully combined. The dough should be firm without sticking to your hands.

Divide the dough into thirds, then roll out each piece into a long sausage roughly 1cm thick. Slice each sausage into 3cm pieces so you're left with 30 or so gnocchi. Gently roll each gnocchi down the back of a fork along its prongs. This will create those famous grooves.

Bring the reserved potato cooking water back to the boil, adding more boiling water if necessary, then add the gnocchi and cook for a few minutes. The gnocchi are cooked when they rise to the top, so get ready with a slotted spoon and transfer them to a colander.

Season the spicy sauce to taste, then add the cooked gnocchi and stir until completely coated in the sauce.

Serve with a sprinkling of chopped basil and a drizzle of extra virgin olive oil, then garnish with a couple of small basil leaves.

BROCCOLI ALFREDO

We always have a supply of cashews ready to use for a creamy sauce. Here we blend them with nutritional yeast aka 'nooch' to replace the heavy cream used in traditional Alfredos.

Serves 2

70g raw cashews
150g tagliatelle
200g Tenderstem broccoli
2 garlic cloves
3 tbsp nutritional yeast

Transfer the cashews to a small bowl and soak them in hot water from the kettle for 10 minutes.

Add a pinch of salt to a pan of boiling water set over a high heat and cook the tagliatelle as per the packet instructions.

Meanwhile, add a little olive oil to a frying pan over a medium heat. Once hot, trim any leaves off the broccoli, add the broccoli to the pan and fry for 8 minutes, until tender, stirring occasionally. Peel and dice the garlic, then add to the pan and fry for a further 2 minutes.

Drain the pasta, reserving the pasta water in a measuring jug. Return the cooked pasta to the saucepan and leave to one side.

Drain the cashews and add them to a blender along with the nutritional yeast, 150ml of the reserved pasta water and 1 teaspoon of apple cider vinegar. Blend until smooth, then season with a pinch of salt and pepper. We usually add a generous amount of pepper because it gives the sauce a lovely warm kick, but trust your own palate and season to taste.

Pour the creamy sauce into the saucepan with the pasta, then add the broccoli and garlic. Mix everything together.

Serve in a bowl, then drizzle the pasta mixture with a splash of extra virgin olive oil to finish.

TIP

Don't forget, you can use that
(cooled) leftover nutrient-rich
pasta water to feed your plants!

⏱ **Prep** 25 mins   ⏱ **Cook** 45 mins   💷   Ir Ca

BUTTERNUT SQUASH NAAN BREADS

Serves 2

350g butternut squash
130g self-raising flour,
   plus extra for dusting
130g coconut soya yoghurt,
   plus extra for serving
1½ tbsp madras curry paste
80g fresh spinach

The best thing about these awesome little naans is they're so easy to make. We use two ingredients to create a lovely sweet bread, which we then coat in a spicy butternut squash paste. These are fun, tasty and they'll definitely impress your friends.

Preheat the oven to 220°C/200°C fan/gas mark 7 and line a baking tray with baking paper.

Peel the butternut squash, discard the seeds and cut into 3cm chunks. Place the squash chunks on another (unlined) baking tray, drizzle with olive oil and season with salt and pepper. Bake in the oven for 30 minutes, until tender.

Meanwhile, make the dough by mixing the flour, yoghurt and ½ teaspoon of salt together in a large mixing bowl. Transfer the dough to a well-floured surface and knead for 1 minute. Add more flour if the dough is too sticky, or add more yoghurt if it's too dry. The consistency will depend on what yoghurt you use, but it should be the same as bread dough.

Divide the dough in half and flour a rolling pin. Roll each half into an oval shape roughly 5mm thick, then transfer each naan dough to the lined baking tray and leave to one side.

When the butternut squash is ready, remove it from the oven and leave to cool for 5 minutes. Add the butternut squash to a food processor along with the madras curry paste and 1 tablespoon of cold water. Process until smooth.

Spread the butternut squash paste over both naans, then bake in the oven for 15 minutes.

Meanwhile, wilt the spinach with a splash of cold water in a saucepan over a medium heat for about 4–6 minutes, stirring occasionally, then drain off the excess water.

Remove the naans from the oven and top with the wilted spinach, a few dollops of extra yoghurt, some grinds of pepper and a drizzle of extra virgin olive oil. Then tuck in!

'We spend so much time testing recipes to make sure they're perfect, so we're lucky to have friends who often pop over and hoover it all up!'

DEEP-PAN PIZZA

We thought pizza would be the hardest thing to give up when we decided to go vegan. Then we realised we could just make it ourselves! This classic deep pan version is indulgent and ridiculously satisfying.

Makes 1 medium pizza

230g plain flour,
    plus extra for dusting
1 tsp fast-action dried yeast
small handful of fresh basil,
    plus extra to garnish
150g tomato purée
150g vegan mozzarella

Mix the flour, yeast and ½ teaspoon of salt together in a large mixing bowl, creating a well in the middle. Pour 150ml of tepid water into the well along with 1 tablespoon of olive oil, then use a spoon to mix everything together into a sticky ball.

Transfer the dough to a floured surface and knead for 5 minutes, adding pinches of flour as you go to prevent the dough sticking to your hands or the surface.

Place the dough into a lightly greased mixing bowl, cover with a clean tea towel and leave it to prove somewhere warm for at least an hour. The dough should double in size.

Preheat the oven to 240ºC/220ºC fan/gas mark 9.

Gently punch the dough a few times to push the air out and transfer it to a floured surface, then roll the dough out into a circle roughly 35cm in diameter. Lightly grease a 25cm ovenproof frying pan, then add the pizza dough to the pan so it covers the base and falls slightly over the edges.

Roughly chop the basil and add it to a small bowl along with the tomato purée, 80ml of cold water, 2 teaspoons of apple cider vinegar and a generous pinch of salt and pepper. Stir the sauce to combine, then spoon it over the pizza base. Trim any excess dough that is hanging over the edge of the pan, then fold the sides in on themselves to create a thick crust.

Slice the mozzarella and spread it out evenly on top of the sauce. Bake in the oven for 15–25 minutes or until the crust turns a light brown.

To finish, drizzle the pizza with a splash of extra virgin olive oil, top with a few extra grinds of pepper and garnish with a few basil leaves.

Tip
Make sure the yeast is fresh! Old dried yeast will become inactive and your dough won't rise.

CREAMY SPINACH RAVIOLI

A delicious ravioli in just five ingredients. Yes, you read that correctly! We're so proud of these little beauties and we always parade them in front of our friends.

Serves 2

120g raw cashews,
    plus extra to garnish
60g fresh spinach
150g plain flour,
    plus extra for dusting
1 lemon
large handful of fresh basil,
    plus extra for serving

In a small bowl, soak the cashews in hot water directly from the kettle, while you work through the next few steps.

Blanch the spinach in boiling water for a couple of minutes until soft, then strain it, reserving the leftover water. Transfer the spinach to a small blender, add 3 tablespoons of the reserved spinach water and blend until smooth. If you don't have a small blender, you can use a handheld one to blend everything together in a bowl.

Next, add the flour to a large mixing bowl along with a generous pinch of salt. Make a well in the middle, pour in the blitzed spinach, then mix everything together. Transfer the dough to a floured surface and knead for 5 minutes, then wrap it tightly in baking paper and refrigerate for 30 minutes.

Divide the chilled pasta dough in half and roll each piece out until it's as thin as you can get it without splitting the dough (this should be around 2mm). Use a pastry cutter 8cm in diameter or the rim of a pint glass to cut the dough into circles. Repeat until all of the dough is used up and you're left with 20 circles.

Drain the cashews and add them to a blender along with the juice from the lemon, basil and 3 tablespoons of cold water. Blend until the mixture reaches a smooth but thick consistency, then season well with salt and pepper. Add a heaped tablespoon of the cashew mixture to the centre of a pasta circle and cover it with another circle. Use your thumb to press down around the edges, sealing the circles together. To finish, use the prongs of a fork to pinch all around the edges. Repeat until you're left with 10 filled ravioli.

Bring a saucepan of water to the boil and cook the ravioli for 5 minutes, until tender, then carefully scoop out using a slotted spoon. We usually cook the ravioli in two batches to avoid them sticking together.

Meanwhile, finely slice half a dozen or so basil leaves and mix them in a small bowl with 2 tablespoons of extra virgin olive oil. Drizzle the oil over the ravioli and sprinkle a few cashews on top to serve.

WHOLE-ROASTED CAULIFLOWER KORMA

Serves 3–4

400ml tin full-fat coconut milk
2 tbsp korma paste
1 large cauliflower
handful of fresh coriander
handful of raisins

Cauliflower is one of those veggies that will happily take centre stage at any dinner table. The korma paste and coconut is a match made in heaven; it's creamy, sweet and has all the wonderful aromas you'd expect from a curry. We'll usually serve this alongside rice and a bowl of wilted spinach.

Open the tin of coconut milk to check if the cream has set. If not, place the tin in the fridge until the cream has set to the top, then preheat the oven to 220ºC/200ºC fan/gas mark 7.

Scoop out the coconut cream into a bowl and set to one side. In a separate bowl, add 2 tablespoons of the coconut water from the tin (save the rest because you'll need it later) along with 1 tablespoon of the korma paste, 1 tablespoon of olive oil and a pinch of salt and pepper.

Remove the leaves from the cauliflower and cut a deep cross in the base of the stalk. Place the cauliflower on a baking tray and use a brush to rub the korma coconut sauce all over it. Roast in the oven for 50 minutes.

A few minutes before the cauliflower has finished cooking, add 100ml of the remaining coconut water to a saucepan along with the remaining 1 tablespoon of korma paste and 2 tablespoons of the coconut cream you saved earlier.

Cook the sauce over a medium heat for a few minutes until hot, stirring occasionally, then pour it over the roasted cauliflower.

Roughly chop the coriander, then top the cauliflower with the remaining coconut cream, followed by the coriander and the raisins. Epic.

Tip
Remember to use full-fat coconut milk (with a high fat content), because you need the cream to set at the top of the tin.

MUSHROOM, SAGE & ONION WELLINGTON

Serves 4

8 portobello mushrooms
3 onions
10 fresh sage leaves
120g walnuts
2 x 320g sheets of
    dairy-free puff pastry

Tip
Did you know most store-bought pastry is vegan? You should always check the label, but you'll be pleasantly surprised at how easy it is to get your hands on some quality ready-made pastry.

This is an absolute showstopper. We'll make this wellington for friends on a Sunday afternoon, alongside our Rosemary & Thyme Roast Potatoes (see page 193) and Brussels Sprouts (see page 216).

Preheat the oven to 220°C/200°C fan/gas mark 7 and line a large baking tray with baking paper.

Wipe any excess dirt off the mushrooms and place 5 of them in an ovenproof dish. Drizzle with olive oil and season with salt and pepper, then bake in the oven for 15 minutes. Then remove the mushrooms from the oven and set aside, leaving the oven switched on for later.

Meanwhile, quarter the remaining mushrooms, then peel and roughly chop the onions and add both to a food processor along with sage leaves, walnuts, ½ teaspoon of salt and 1 teaspoon of pepper. Process to form a smooth paste, then add to a frying pan over a medium-high heat and fry for 15 minutes, stirring frequently. Set aside to cool for 10 minutes.

Roll out 1 sheet of pastry onto the lined baking tray. Spread a third of the paste down the middle of the pastry lengthways, spreading it 5cm wide and leaving 5cm clear at each end.

Turn the baked mushrooms upside down to remove any excess juices, then place 3 of the mushrooms, gills facing up, on top of the paste down the middle of the pastry. Add the remaining 2 mushrooms, gills facing down, between the 3 mushrooms. Spoon the remaining paste around the mushrooms to cover them on all sides.

Place the second sheet of pastry on top and use your fingers to seal the edges together. Trim around the wellington roughly 1cm away from the filling, discarding the excess pastry as you go. Lightly score the wellington with diagonal lines at 3cm intervals and brush with olive oil. Bake in the oven for 50 minutes, until the pastry turns a lovely golden brown.

Remove from the oven and serve in slices.

SUPER SQUASH TRAY BAKE

We love a tray bake. It's a healthy way to cook veggies and there's hardly any washing up to do when you're done. We love the flavours in this dish. It's tangy, sweet and earthy, and it's packed with lots of the nutrients your body needs.

Serves 2

1 butternut squash
10 fresh sage leaves
400g tin green lentils
2 tsp Dijon mustard
2 handfuls of rocket

Preheat the oven to 200°C/180°C fan/gas mark 6.

Slice the butternut squash in half, then trim and discard the ends and spoon out the seeds (see Tip). Cut the butternut squash into 1cm-thick pieces and transfer to a large baking tray along with 2 tablespoons of olive oil, ½ teaspoon of salt and ½ teaspoon of pepper.

Finely chop the sage leaves (you'll need about 2 tablespoons) and sprinkle over the squash pieces. Combine everything with your hands, then bake in the oven for 35–45 minutes until tender.

Remove the baking tray from the oven. Drain and rinse the lentils, then add to the squash and mix lightly. Return to the oven and bake for a further 10 minutes.

Meanwhile, prepare the dressing by combining the mustard in a small bowl with 2 tablespoons of extra virgin olive oil, 1 teaspoon of apple cider vinegar and a pinch of salt and pepper.

Remove the squash and lentil mixture from the oven and divide between 2 serving plates. Top each serving with a handful of rocket and then finish with a generous drizzle of the mustard dressing.

Tip
Instead of throwing the butternut squash seeds in the bin, wash the seeds, then roast them with your favourite seasoning to create a healthy snack.

🕐 **Prep** 15 mins   🕐 **Cook** 25 mins   £ £   Ir Pr

PEANUT BUTTER TOFU ZOODLES

This has everything you'd want from a big bowl of noodles. It's spicy, salty and healthy, so there's a lot going on to keep your taste buds happy. We love to use courgette instead of regular noodles for some added nutrition and colour.

Serves 2

250g extra-firm tofu
60g dry roasted peanuts,
    plus extra to garnish
2 tbsp chilli garlic sauce
1 tbsp white granulated sugar
2 large courgettes

Press the tofu to remove any excess water, then slice it into 3cm pieces. Add a little olive oil to a frying pan over a medium heat. Once hot, add the tofu and fry for 15–20 minutes, turning every 5 minutes, so that both sides get crispy.

Meanwhile, add the peanuts, chilli garlic sauce, sugar, 2 tablespoons of olive oil, 1 teaspoon of apple cider vinegar and 6 tablespoons of cold water to a food processor. Blend everything together to create a smooth sauce, then pour the sauce into a bowl and, if needed, season with salt and pepper. The sauce will already be quite salty, so we usually avoid adding extra salt.

When the tofu is ready, remove it from the pan and drop the tofu pieces into the peanut sauce, making sure they're coated all over.

Add a small splash of olive oil into the same pan you used earlier and reduce the heat to low. Add the coated tofu pieces back into the pan and fry for a couple of minutes, turning occasionally.

Meanwhile, use a spiraliser to cut the courgettes into thin noodle-like spirals (see Tip).

Remove the tofu from the pan and set to one side in a bowl. Add the courgette to the frying pan and pour in any remaining peanut sauce along with 1 tablespoon of cold water. Fry for 2 minutes, stirring occasionally.

Serve by placing the courgette noodles on a plate, cover with the tofu, then sprinkle some crushed peanuts on top.

Tip
If you don't have a spiraliser, don't fret. You can simply slice the courgettes into long thin sticks for a similar effect.

LOADED SWEET POTATOES

This is something we'll often turn to when we're both too busy to spend hours in the kitchen. We leave the sweet spuds to bake in the oven, then simply throw everything together in the last few minutes. If you have the time, have a go at creating our Lemon & Coriander Hummus (see page 234).

Serves 2

2 medium sweet potatoes
400g tin chickpeas
2 tsp ground cumin
5 tbsp hummus
large handful of fresh
    flat-leaf parsley

Preheat the oven to 220°C/200°C fan/gas mark 7.

Rinse and pat dry the sweet potatoes, then pierce them a few times with a fork. Place them on a baking tray and bake in the oven for 40–50 minutes or until soft throughout.

When the sweet potatoes have 5 minutes left in the oven, drizzle a little olive oil into a frying pan set over a medium-high heat. Drain and rinse the chickpeas, then once the oil is hot add them to the frying pan along with the cumin, a generous pinch of salt and pepper and 2 tablespoons of cold water. Fry for 5 minutes, stirring frequently.

Meanwhile, prepare the dressing by combining the hummus with 2 tablespoons of cold water in a small bowl, until smooth.

Remove the sweet potatoes from the oven and place on serving plates. Cut them in half and fill each potato with half of the chickpea mixture, then generously drizzle the hummus dressing over the top. Roughly chop the parsley and sprinkle on top to serve.

ARTICHOKE & TAPENADE PASTA

This artichoke and tapenade pasta is really quick and easy to put together, and it's something we'll constantly turn to when we're working late on So Vegan.

Serves 2

200g conchiglioni (or similar)
100g artichokes in oil,
**   plus 1 tbsp oil from the jar**
250g ripe cherry tomatoes
2 tbsp black olive tapenade
2 tbsp grated vegan parmesan

Add a pinch of salt to a pan of boiling water set over a high heat and cook the pasta as per the packet instructions.

Halve the cherry tomatoes and roughly chop the artichokes. Add the oil from the jar of artichokes to a frying pan over a medium heat. Once it's hot, add the cherry tomato halves and artichoke pieces. Fry for 8 minutes, stirring occasionally.

Drain the pasta, reserving the cooking water in a measuring jug. Add the pasta to the tomatoes and artichokes in the frying pan, then add 4 tablespoons of the reserved pasta water along with the tapenade, a generous pinch of salt and pepper and 1 tablespoon of the grated parmesan. Stir to combine.

To serve, drizzle the pasta mixture with a splash of extra virgin olive oil and sprinkle with the remaining parmesan.

Tip
You'll find vegan parmesan in big supermarkets, or you can make your own using our recipe (see page 266).

MINCED MUSHROOM TACOS

Makes 6 tacos

½ red onion
600g chestnut mushrooms
2½ tbsp cajun seasoning
200g ripe tomatoes
6 small flour tortillas

Nowadays 'date night' involves staying indoors, rustling up these awesome tacos, and Roxy falling asleep on the sofa while we watch a film. We love using cajun; we find it has more depth compared to other spice mixes and it adds a wonderfully warm kick to the mushrooms.

Preheat the oven to 200°C/180°C fan/gas mark 6.

Thinly slice the red onion and add to a bowl along with 1 tablespoon of apple cider vinegar and a pinch of salt. Mix everything together and leave the onion to pickle away, while you crack on with the remaining steps.

Add the mushrooms to a food processor and pulse until no big pieces remain. Add the mushroom 'mince' to a large baking tray, drizzle with 1 tablespoon of olive oil and add a generous pinch of salt and pepper. Bake in the oven for 20 minutes.

Remove from the oven, stir the cajun seasoning into the mushrooms, then return to the oven and bake for a further 10 minutes.

Meanwhile, dice the tomatoes and add them to a bowl along with a pinch of salt and pepper and a light drizzle of extra virgin olive oil. Stir to combine, then leave to one side.

Heat a frying pan over a medium heat. When the pan is hot, toast each tortilla for 45–60 seconds on each side, until they begin to char.

Build each taco by adding a few tablespoons of minced mushrooms to a tortilla, then top with 1 tablespoon of diced tomatoes and a small handful of the pickled red onion.

APRICOT & ROSEMARY NUT ROAST

Serves 4, generously

2 onions
200g dried apricots
200g mixed nuts
400g tin green lentils
4 fresh rosemary sprigs

Long before we were vegan, we would insist on making a nut roast for a Sunday dinner, so we just knew we had to include one in this cookbook. The apricot and rosemary is such a winning combo, and we bet even the meat eaters will approve.

Preheat the oven to 200°C/180°C fan/gas mark 6 and line a 450g (approx. 20 x 10cm) loaf tin with baking paper.

Heat a little olive oil in a frying pan over a medium heat. Peel and finely dice the onion, then fry for 10 minutes, until softened, stirring frequently.

Meanwhile, add the apricots to a food processor along with 100ml of cold water and process until it forms a smooth paste. Add the nuts and pulse until they have mostly broken down. Drain and rinse the lentils, then add to the food processor and pulse everything again until the mixture holds together. Transfer the mixture to a large mixing bowl.

Pull the rosemary leaves off the stalks, chop the leaves (you should be left with roughly 2 tablespoons) and add them to the mixing bowl along with the fried onions, ½ teaspoon of salt and ½ teaspoon of pepper, then mix everything together.

Transfer the mixture to the prepared loaf tin, pushing it down into the tin as you go, so it's compact and level. Bake in the oven for 45 minutes, until golden brown.

Remove from the oven and leave the nut roast to stand in the tin for 5 minutes, before turning it out onto a wooden board. Serve in slices.

🕐 **Prep** 15 mins   🕐 **Cook** 30 mins   💷 💷

PULLED BBQ MUSHROOM BURGERS

There's nobody more obsessed with mushrooms than our friend Derek Sarno from Wicked Healthy. Inspired loosely by Derek, our version uses shitake mushrooms and we throw them together with cajun seasoning and BBQ sauce, then top with gherkins for that satisfying crunch.

Serves 2

250g shiitake mushrooms
1½ tbsp cajun seasoning
2 tbsp BBQ sauce,
     plus extra for serving
2 ciabatta rolls
2 large pickled gherkins

Preheat the oven to 200°C/180°C fan/gas mark 6.

Brush any dirt off the mushrooms, then shred them apart on a chopping board using your hands or a fork. The stalks will pull apart into shreds and you'll need to use the side of the fork to break down the cups into 5mm-thick strips.

Add the shredded mushrooms to a baking tray, drizzle with a splash of olive oil and season with a generous pinch of salt. Mix everything together with your hands and then bake in the oven for 25 minutes.

Remove from the oven. Add the cajun seasoning and BBQ sauce to the mushrooms, mix everything up again and return to the oven for a further 5 minutes.

Meanwhile, slice the ciabatta rolls in half and toast them on a griddle pan for a couple of minutes until lightly brown.

Now it's time to build the burgers. Spread half of the pulled mushrooms on the bottom half of each ciabatta roll. Slice the gherkins and add 4–5 slices on top, followed by some extra BBQ sauce to each, then top with the other halves of the ciabatta rolls. Enjoy!

Tip
Choose shiitake mushrooms with long stalks, so you'll end up with more of that awesome shredded texture.

SPINACH & TOFU FILO PIE

We love serving this for weekend lunch with friends or family. It's light and crispy, and the subtle flavours all come together to create a brilliantly satisfying meal. Serve alongside our Parsley & Mint Chickpea Salad (see page 199) for the perfect Mediterranean match.

Serves 6

300g fresh spinach
560g extra-firm tofu
100g sun-dried tomatoes in oil (from a jar)
6 tbsp nutritional yeast
6 sheets of dairy-free filo pastry

Preheat the oven to 200°C/180°C fan/gas mark 6 and grease a 20cm round springform cake tin with olive oil.

Add the spinach to a large bowl, cover with hot water from the kettle and leave to wilt for 2 minutes. Meanwhile, squeeze any excess water out of the tofu and crumble it into a large mixing bowl, until no big pieces remain.

Add the sun-dried tomatoes and 3 tablespoons of oil from the jar to a food processor and process until finely chopped, then add to the large mixing bowl with the tofu, along with the nutritional yeast, 1 teaspoon of salt and 1 teaspoon of pepper. Drain the spinach through a sieve, pressing out any excess water, then add it to the bowl and stir everything together until combined.

Add a sheet of filo pastry to the prepared springform tin so that the ends hang over the edge of the tin, then brush the sheet with olive oil. Turn the tin about 60 degrees clockwise and add another sheet of filo pastry and brush with olive oil. Repeat the process, turning the tin 60 degrees each time and brushing the pastry with oil, until all of the pastry sheets have been used up and the tin is totally covered.

Add the tofu mixture to the pastry case, spreading it out evenly. Fold in the edges of the pastry sheets one at a time, starting with the last sheet that was put in and working in reverse order, brushing the pastry tops with olive oil as you go. Transfer the filo pie to the oven and bake for 30 minutes or until crisp and golden brown.

Remove the sides of the tin and gently transfer the pie to a chopping board to serve.

⏱ **Prep** 15 mins ⏱ **Cook** 40 mins £

PURPLE LINGUINE

This is a stunning plate of food. Roxy grew up on a diet of beetroot in all shapes and sizes, thanks to her Polish mum. Here we combine it with dill for a winning flavour combo, while delivering an incredibly deep purple colour, which makes this dish so warm and inviting.

Serves 2

2 medium raw beetroots
200g linguine
handful of fresh dill,
    plus extra to garnish
½ lemon
4 tbsp single soya cream

Preheat the oven to 200°C/180°C fan/gas mark 6.

Peel the beetroot, trim the ends and cut into 2cm chunks. Place the beetroot chunks on a baking tray, drizzle with olive oil and season with salt and pepper, then use your hands to combine everything. Bake in the oven for 30 minutes.

Remove from the oven and leave the beetroot to cool slightly, while you cook the pasta.

Add a pinch of salt to a saucepan of boiling water set over a high heat and cook the pasta as per the packet instructions.

Drain the pasta, reserving the cooking water in a measuring jug, then return the pasta to the saucepan and set to one side.

Add the beetroot, dill, juice of the lemon, soya cream, a generous pinch of salt, ½ teaspoon of pepper and 125ml of the reserved pasta water to a food processor, and process until smooth.

Add the beetroot sauce to the pasta, stirring to coat the pasta until it becomes an amazing purple colour.

Serve with a drizzle of extra virgin olive oil and a sprinkling of chopped dill.

RATATOUILLE SWIRL

The trick to impressing friends is creating something that looks and tastes epic, but is actually a total breeze in the kitchen. Step forward our Ratatouille Swirl, which we enjoy serving alongside our homemade Olive & Rosemary Focaccia (see page 205).

Serves 4

500ml tomato and
    basil pasta sauce
2 garlic cloves
2 medium, thin aubergines
1 large courgette
4 ripe plum tomatoes

Preheat the oven to 200°C/180°C fan/gas mark 6.

Pour the pasta sauce into a 25cm ovenproof frying pan or round dish, then finely chop the garlic and stir it into the sauce.

Slice the aubergines, courgette and tomatoes into 3mm-thick rounds, discarding the tops of the aubergines and courgette as you go. Pick up a slice of each vegetable and arrange the stack of 3 slices around the inside edge of the pan or dish on top of the pasta sauce, to create a compact spiral shape. Repeat until you create a swirl, covering the entire inside of the pan.

Use a brush to coat the top of the vegetables with a little olive oil, then sprinkle a generous pinch of salt and pepper on top.

Cover the ratatouille swirl with foil and bake in the oven for 30 minutes. Remove from the oven, discard the foil and return the swirl to the oven to bake for a further 30 minutes.

Remove from the oven and leave the ratatouille swirl to rest for 10 minutes or so before serving.

Tip
You can use normal medium-sized tomatoes if you're struggling to find the plum variety.

Prep 15 mins   **Cook** 20–25 mins

ZA'ATAR CAULIFLOWER STEAKS

Makes 2 steaks

½ tbsp za'atar
1 large cauliflower
1 garlic clove
2 tbsp tahini
½ pomegranate

We seriously can't get enough of za'atar. This aromatic blend of spices has pride of place in our cupboard and it carries such a unique flavour. Tangy and zesty, it pairs fantastically with a variety of veggies, none more so than the trusted cauliflower.

Preheat the oven to 220ºC/200ºC fan/gas mark 7 and line a large baking tray with baking paper.

In a small bowl, combine the za'atar with 2 tablespoons of olive oil and a pinch of salt and pepper.

Rinse and pat dry the cauliflower, then remove the leaves, reserving them for later, and trim the stalk end so the cauliflower stands upright. You'll only need the chunky middle part of the cauliflower, so trim 2 opposite sides, then cut the remainder in half through the stalk to make 2 'steaks' (see Tip for how to use the leftover cauli).

Place the 2 cauliflower steaks on the lined baking tray and brush all the sides with the za'atar dressing. Bake in the oven for 10–15 minutes.

Remove from the oven, place the outer cauli leaves on the baking tray and drizzle them with a little olive oil. Return to the oven and bake for a further 10 minutes.

Meanwhile, peel and finely dice the garlic, then add it to a small bowl along with the tahini, 3 tablespoons of cold water and a small pinch of salt and pepper. Stir to combine then set to one side.

Prepare the pomegranate by holding the pomegranate half over a mixing bowl and tapping the skin sharply with a wooden spoon to release the seeds.

Place each cauliflower steak with a few leaves on a plate, then serve with a generous drizzle of tahini sauce and a sprinkling of pomegranate seeds.

TIP

Grate the leftover cauliflower,
add your favourite seasoning,
then fry it gently for 5 minutes
to make cauliflower rice.

THE CARNIVAL TOFU BURGER

We're really proud of this nifty burger. It took on various forms until we settled on using jerk BBQ sauce and plantain. It's sweet, sticky and satisfyingly filling.

Serves 2

300g extra-firm tofu
4 tbsp jerk BBQ sauce
3 burger buns
1 ripe plantain
2 handfuls of crunchy
   lettuce leaves

Preheat the oven to 140°C/120°C fan/gas mark 1.

Squeeze out any excess water from the tofu and slice it into 4 rectangles, each roughly 1cm thick, then transfer to a plate. Brush 2 tablespoons of the jerk BBQ sauce over the tofu, until it's completely covered, then leave it to marinate in the fridge, while you prepare the breadcrumbs.

Tear one of the burger buns into pieces, add it to a food processor and pulse until it breaks down into small crumbs. Pour the crumbs out evenly onto a baking tray and bake in the oven for 5–10 minutes, until lightly brown.

Remove the breadcrumbs from the oven and set aside. Increase the oven temperature to 200°C/180°C fan/gas mark 6 and line a separate baking tray with baking paper.

Take each slice of marinated tofu and press it in the breadcrumbs, making sure the tofu is completely coated on all sides. Transfer the coated tofu pieces to the lined baking tray and bake for 15–20 minutes, until golden brown.

Meanwhile, prepare the plantain by peeling it and slicing the flesh into diagonal pieces about 2cm thick. Season with a pinch of salt, then fry the plantain slices in a little olive oil in a frying pan over a medium heat for 2–3 minutes on each side, until lightly coloured and soft.

In the meantime, halve the remaining burger buns and toast them, face down, on a griddle pan over a high heat for a couple of minutes, until they begin to brown.

Build the burgers by first adding a handful of crunchy lettuce leaves on top of each bottom bun, followed by 2 slices of tofu and half of the plantain. Spoon a tablespoon of the remaining jerk BBQ sauce on top, then cover with the top half of each bun. Tuck in!

Tip
Make sure the plantain is ripe! It will be a lot sweeter and will add tons more flavour to the burgers.

DESSERTS

PEAR & CHOCOLATE CAKE

This epic pudding took on various shapes and sizes before we finally settled on what you now see before you. We wanted to create something that not only looks the part, but totally tastes the part.

Serves 10

5 ripe pears
225g self-raising flour
60g cocoa powder, plus 2 tbsp
200g white caster sugar, plus
    2 tbsp, plus extra for sprinkling
150ml coconut oil, melted, plus
    1 tbsp, plus extra for greasing

Preheat the oven to 200°C/180°C fan/gas mark 6. Grease a 23cm-round springform cake tin with coconut oil and line the base of the tin with baking paper.

Peel 2 of the pears, remove the cores and cut the flesh into small pieces. Add the pear pieces to a small saucepan over a medium heat along with 2 tablespoons of cold water, then simmer for 10 minutes until the pear is soft, stirring occasionally.

Remove from the heat and mash the pear with a fork or potato masher to form a purée.

Add the flour, the 60g of cocoa powder, the 200g of sugar and a pinch of salt to a large mixing bowl, and stir to combine. Create a well in the middle and add the pear purée, the 150ml of melted coconut oil and 4 tablespoons of cold water, then stir together until smooth and combined. Pour the cake mixture into the prepared springform tin, then shake the tin to level the mixture.

Peel and halve the remaining 3 pears, then remove the cores. Arrange the pear halves, cut side down, on top of the cake mixture, equal distances apart. Brush them with olive oil and sprinkle with extra caster sugar. Bake in the oven for 45–50 minutes or until a toothpick or fine skewer comes out clean when inserted into the cake.

Remove from the oven, leave the cake to cool in the tin for 5 minutes, then remove the sides of the tin and carefully slide the cake onto a serving plate.

Prepare the chocolate drizzle by melting together the remaining 2 tablespoons of cocoa powder, 2 tablespoons of caster sugar and 1 tablespoon of coconut oil with 2 tablespoons of cold water in a small saucepan over a low heat until combined, then drizzle this all over the cake. Serve warm in slices. Yum!

Tip
It's really important that you use perfectly ripe pears, otherwise you'll miss out on all their gorgeous sweetness.

MINI PASSION FRUIT PAVLOVAS

Who said vegans can't eat pavlova? We use a secret ingredient to create these beautiful little desserts. Aquafaba is the liquid drained from a tin of chickpeas and it doubles up as an egg replacer in this vegan pavlova.

Makes 12 mini pavlovas

80ml aquafaba (from a tin of unsalted chickpeas)
50g white caster sugar
2 passion fruit
4 tbsp coconut yoghurt
36 or so fresh raspberries

Preheat the oven to 120°C/100°C fan/gas mark ½ and line a large baking tray with baking paper.

Using an electric whisk, whisk the aquafaba and ¼ teaspoon of apple cider vinegar together in a mixing bowl, until you get stiff peaks. This should take roughly 8 minutes. You'll know when it's ready because you'll be able to turn the bowl upside down without the mixture falling out.

Add the sugar, a couple of tablespoons at a time, and continue whisking for roughly 3 minutes until it's all incorporated.

Pipe or spoon the mixture into 4cm-diameter circles directly onto the lined baking tray. Bake in the oven for 2 hours.

Turn the oven off and leave the meringues in the oven for another hour so they remain firm.

Remove the meringues from the oven and leave them to cool completely.

Meanwhile, cut the passion fruit in half, scoop out the flesh and place it in a small bowl ready to use for the topping.

Carefully peel the cold meringues off the baking paper. Top each meringue with a teaspoon of coconut yoghurt, a drizzle of passion fruit pulp and a few raspberries. Serve immediately.

Tip
After you've used the aquafaba, you can put the chickpeas to work in our classic hummus recipes (see pages 225, 234–235).

MINT CHOC CHIP ICE CREAM

You won't need to splash out on an ice-cream maker to recreate this awesome dessert. We use powdered green tea, called matcha, which is not only high in nutrients and antioxidants, it also gives the ice cream its gorgeous green colour. Matcha doesn't always come cheap, but you can put it to good use in muffins or pestos, or simply enjoy a cup of good old matcha tea.

Serves 3

400ml tin coconut milk
1 tsp matcha powder
1 tsp peppermint extract
2 tbsp agave syrup,
     plus extra for serving
100g dairy-free dark-
     chocolate chips

Add the coconut milk, matcha powder, peppermint extract, agave syrup and a pinch of salt to a food processor and blend until smooth.

Pour the mixture into ice-cube moulds and transfer to the freezer. Freeze overnight.

Remove from the freezer and transfer the cubes of ice cream to a food processor. Process until the mixture becomes soft like ice cream. The mixture might seem grainy at first, but keep going until it reaches a smooth consistency.

Remove the blade from the processor and stir in the chocolate chips. Serve immediately with a drizzle of agave syrup.

Tip
Most dark-chocolate chips will be vegan-friendly, but it's always worth checking the ingredients on the packet to be absolutely sure.

COCONUT CHOCOLATE BARS

We love making food that reminds us of our childhood and these coconut chocolate bars are like a nostalgic trip down memory lane. The pistachios bring a colourful crunch, but you can add your own twist with your favourite toppings.

Makes 8 bars

400ml tin full-fat coconut milk
120g desiccated coconut
5 tbsp golden syrup
150g dairy-free dark chocolate
25g pistachios

Open the tin of coconut milk to check if the cream has set. If not, place the tin in the fridge for 1 hour.

When the coconut cream has set at the top of the tin, scoop out 150g of the cream and transfer it to a mixing bowl along with the desiccated coconut, golden syrup and a pinch of salt. Stir until everything is fully combined.

Mould the mixture into 8 mini bars, then place the bars on a freezerproof tray, transfer to the freezer and freeze for 1 hour to firm up.

Meanwhile, prepare the pistachios for decoration by peeling the shells and roughly chopping the nuts. Set to one side for later.

Break up the chocolate and add to a heatproof bowl set over a pan of gently simmering water (make sure the bottom of the bowl doesn't come into contact with the water underneath), then stir the chocolate occasionally until it has completely melted.

Remove the bars from the freezer and coat them in the melted chocolate, one at a time, using a couple of metal spoons to guide the chocolate over the bars. Transfer the bars to a wire rack (set over a sheet of baking paper, to catch any drips) and sprinkle with the pistachios. Leave to set before serving.

Tip
Try our 'shake test' when you buy tinned coconut milk. We avoid buying tins that sound slushy when you shake them, because this might mean the cream won't set in the fridge.

'One of the best feelings ever

is seeing people all over the world recreate our recipes at home.'

MANGO & PEACH SORBET

We've learned to truly appreciate a delicious sorbet since becoming vegan. They're always a refreshing sight on restaurant menus because most of the time they'll be vegan-friendly! This mango and peach version is a great palate cleanser after a rich meal and a healthier way to enjoy a sweet dessert.

Serves 4

2 ripe mangoes
3 ripe peaches
125ml tinned coconut milk
    (stirred well to combine
    the cream and water)
1 tbsp agave syrup,
    plus extra for serving
1 lime

Peel and stone the mangoes, then slice the flesh. Add most of the slices to a freezerproof container and freeze overnight, leaving a few slices in the fridge to use as decoration (see Tip).

When you're ready to make the sorbet, submerge the peaches in a bowl of hot water from the kettle for 1 minute. Carefully remove the peaches from the water, peel off the skins and cut the flesh into slices, discarding the stones.

Save a few peach slices for decoration, then add the rest to a food processor along with the coconut milk, agave syrup and juice from the lime.

Add the frozen mango to the food processor. You may need to wait a little for the mango to defrost slightly so you can break it up. Pulse gently at first to break up the mango pieces, then blend until the mixture is smooth and combined.

You can serve the sorbet as it is, or for a firmer consistency, transfer it back to the freezerproof container and freeze for 2 hours, stirring it every 20 minutes or so.

To serve, scoop the sorbet into bowls and top with an extra drizzle of agave syrup, then decorate with the reserved slices of peach and mango, and grate a few shavings of zest from the lime over the top.

Tip
Freeze the mango way in advance so it's good to go when you need it. It will keep well in the freezer for a few months.

BANOFFEE POTS

We're both big fans of the British classic banoffee pie and we simply weren't prepared to give it up when we decided to go vegan! Here we use Medjool dates to create that irresistibly delicious caramel, and we serve them in small glass 'pots' to make them ideal for a dinner party.

Makes 4 banoffee glasses

400ml tin full-fat coconut milk
200g Medjool dates
8 vegan-friendly oat biscuits
2 ripe bananas
20g dairy-free dark chocolate

Open the tin of coconut milk to check if the cream has set. If not, place the tin in the fridge while you prepare the rest of the dessert.

Remove the stones from the dates, add the dates to a small bowl, pour over some hot water from the kettle, and leave to soak for 10 minutes.

Meanwhile, add the biscuits to a food processor and pulse until only a few large pieces remain. Divide the crushed biscuits evenly between 4 short glasses, reserving a small handful for decoration at the end. Wipe clean the processor.

Drain the dates, reserving the soaking water, and add them to the food processor along with 4 tablespoons of the reserved water and a pinch of salt. Blend until the mixture is smooth like caramel, scraping down the sides of the processor as you go to make sure everything is combined. When it's ready, spoon a quarter of the date caramel into each glass.

Peel the bananas, discarding the skin, and slice them into 5mm-thick discs. Add a layer of banana slices to each glass, saving half of the banana slices for another layer.

Scoop out the thick cream from the tin of coconut milk and transfer it to a mixing bowl. Discard the remaining coconut water left in the tin or save it for your next smoothie. Using a whisk or a spoon, whip the coconut cream until it becomes light and fluffy. Add a heaped tablespoon of coconut cream into each glass and use a small spoon to level the tops.

Top with the remaining slices of banana, then finely chop the dark chocolate and sprinkle it on top, along with the remaining biscuit crumbs. Then serve.

BERRY COBBLER

This is our kind of dessert. It's warm and comforting, and it's exactly what we love to eat on a cold winter's evening. But best of all, it's ridiculously easy to make. There's something really satisfying about soaking up the delicious syrup from the berries using the sweet dough. Divine.

Serves 4

500g frozen mixed berries
60g white caster sugar,
    plus 2 tbsp
½ lemon
220g self-raising flour, plus
    2 tbsp, plus extra for dusting
170ml single soya cream,
    plus extra for serving

Preheat the oven to 200°C/180°C fan/gas mark 6.

Add the frozen berries to a 1-litre ovenproof dish along with the 60g of caster sugar, the juice from the lemon and 2 tablespoons of self-raising flour. Mix everything together (you might have to wait a few minutes for the berries to thaw a little).

Prepare the dough by combining the remaining 220g of self-raising flour, remaining 2 tablespoons of caster sugar, a pinch of salt and the soya cream in a mixing bowl to make a dough. Flour your hands and divide and roughly shape the dough into 8 balls, then place them evenly on top of the berries.

Bake in the oven for 25–30 minutes or until the cobbler topping is risen, cooked and golden brown.

Remove the cobbler from the oven and leave it to cool for 10 minutes, before serving with a generous helping of extra soya cream.

SWEET POTATO BROWNIES

The sweet potato really is the star of the show in these awesome brownies. It makes for a gooey, fudgy and utterly irresistible treat, but better still… it's even slightly healthier than your traditional brownie. These never last long in our home.

Makes 9 squares

400g sweet potato
80g coconut oil,
    plus extra for greasing
140g dairy-free dark chocolate
100g self-raising flour
160g golden caster sugar

Peel the sweet potato and cut it into 2cm-thick slices. Add the sweet potato to a steel steamer basket and place it on top of a saucepan of boiling water. Cover with a lid and steam for 20 minutes or until the sweet potato is soft. Set aside to cool slightly.

Preheat the oven to 200ºC/180ºC fan/gas mark 6. Grease a 20 x 20cm square baking tin with coconut oil, then line the bottom of the tin with baking paper.

Add the coconut oil and dark chocolate to a heatproof bowl set over a pan of gently simmering water (make sure the bottom of the bowl doesn't come into contact with the water underneath). Stir the chocolate occasionally until it has melted, then transfer it to a food processor along with the sweet potato, flour, sugar and a pinch of salt. Process until fully combined, then transfer the mixture to the prepared baking tin, spreading it evenly.

Bake in the oven for 35–45 minutes or until a toothpick or fine skewer comes out clean when inserted into the centre.

Remove from the oven and run a knife around the edges of the brownie to make sure it hasn't stuck to the sides. Leave the brownie to cool slightly in the tin, then remove from the tin and cut into 9 squares to serve. Serve warm or cold.

Any leftover brownies will keep in an airtight container for up to 5 days in the fridge.

NO-BAKE LEMON CHEESECAKE

Serves 12

2 x 400ml tin full-fat coconut milk
450g raw cashews
300g vegan-friendly biscuits
100ml maple syrup
5 lemons

This is a rare treat in our home and it's possibly the most indulgent thing in this cookbook. Enjoy.

Open the tins of coconut milk to check if the cream has set. If not, place the tins in the fridge, until the cream has set to the top.

Transfer the cashews to a bowl and cover with hot water from the kettle. Leave to soak for 1 hour.

Prepare the cheesecake base by adding the biscuits, 2 tablespoons of the maple syrup, 2 tablespoons of olive oil and 1 tablespoon of cold water to a food processor, then process until the mixture is fully broken down. Transfer the base mixture to a 23cm-round springform cake tin and use the bottom of a glass to push the biscuit base down, making sure it's level and compact. Set aside.

Drain the cashews and add them to a blender with the zest and juice from 4 of the lemons and the remaining maple syrup. Remove the tins of coconut milk from the fridge and scoop out the cream straight into the blender. Blend until the cheesecake mix is completely smooth and combined.

Pour the cheesecake mix into the cake tin over the biscuit base and shake the tin to level out the mixture. Transfer the cheesecake to the freezer for 2 hours, until it is firm to touch.

Remove the cheesecake from the freezer and leave it at room temperature for 20 minutes before serving.

Meanwhile, prepare the decoration by peeling the remaining lemon and thinly slicing the peel into 1mm-thick strips.

Pop open the springform tin, carefully slide the cheesecake onto a serving plate and decorate with the lemon peel strips. Serve.

Tip
Remember our 'shake test' when buying tinned coconut milk. Always avoid buying tins that sound slushy when you shake them because the cream probably won't set in the fridge!

ZESTY LEMON BISCUITS

These lemon biscuits are light, zesty and sweet; pretty much everything you'd want from a cheeky after-dinner snack. We always have fun decorating these with the icing and coming up with imaginative patterns.

Makes 20 biscuits

135g icing sugar
60g dairy-free margarine
1 tsp vanilla extract
120g plain flour,
    plus extra for dusting
2 lemons

Preheat the oven to 180ºC/160ºC fan/gas mark 4 and line a large baking tray with baking paper.

Cream 40g of the icing sugar with the margarine and vanilla extract in a bowl. Add the flour along with the zest of 1 lemon and mix together to form a dough.

Generously dust a work surface and a rolling pin with flour, then roll out the dough until it's 5mm thick. Use a 5cm-round cutter to stamp out the biscuits, using up all the dough (and re-rolling it, if necessary) until you have 20 biscuits.

Transfer the biscuits to the lined baking tray, leaving a 1cm gap between each biscuit. Bake in the oven for 15 minutes, until pale golden.

Remove from the oven and leave the biscuits to cool completely.

Prepare the icing by combining the remaining icing sugar with the juice from half a lemon in a small bowl. Add the icing to a piping bag and if necessary snip off the end to create a hole approximately 2mm wide.

Drizzle the icing across all of the biscuits in random patterns, then grate over the zest from the remaining lemon. Wait for the icing to set before serving.

These biscuits will keep in an airtight container for up to 5 days.

Prep 15 mins, plus cooling   **Cook** 10–12 mins   £

LAURA'S PEANUT BUTTER & CHOCOLATE COOKIES

Makes 6 cookies

1 ripe banana
120g crunchy peanut butter
2 tbsp plain flour
¼ tsp bicarbonate of soda
50g dairy-free dark chocolate

This is Laura's winning entry from our cookbook competition. We've been hooked on these cookies ever since we first tried them. They're super addictive, incredibly easy to make and they'll melt in your mouth. Thank you, Laura!

Preheat the oven to 200°C/180°C fan/gas mark 6 and line a large baking tray with baking paper.

Peel the banana and add the flesh to a mixing bowl, then mash with a fork until it becomes a purée. Add the peanut butter, flour and bicarbonate of soda to the bowl.

Roughly chop the dark chocolate into small pieces and add to the mixing bowl, then stir everything together to combine. Depending on what peanut butter you use, you may need to add 1 or 2 tablespoons of extra flour to get a mixture that you can work with. The mixture will be sticky, but you should be able to handle it easily.

Divide and roll the mixture into 6 even balls, then place them on the lined baking tray about 6-8cm apart. Push each dough ball down so the cookie dough spreads about 5cm wide.

Bake in the oven for 10–12 minutes, until they are firm to touch. The cookies should still be soft in the middle.

Remove from the oven and leave the cookies to cool slightly on the baking tray before transferring them to a wire rack. Serve warm or cold.

TIP

Did you know bananas can
be a great substitute for eggs in
vegan baking? They add moisture
and help bind the ingredients
together. Try using half a banana
to replace one egg.

TAHINI COFFEE SHAKE

This milkshake is pure heaven. We thought we'd combine some of our favourite things in the world... tahini, coffee, chocolate and ice cream, to create this decadent dessert.

Makes 2 shakes

**2 double shots of coffee, plus coffee
beans for decoration
60g dairy-free dark chocolate
8 scoops dairy-free vanilla ice cream
4 tbsp tahini
vegan squirty cream (optional)**

If you don't have ice cubes in your freezer, pour cold water into an ice-cube tray and leave it to freeze for a few hours or ideally overnight.

Prepare the double shots of coffee and leave them to one side to cool.

Meanwhile, add 40g of the chocolate to a heatproof bowl set over a pan of gently simmering water (make sure the bottom of the bowl doesn't come into contact with the water underneath). Add 2 tablespoons of the coffee and stir to combine. Once the chocolate has melted, use a spoon to smear the mixture around the inside of 2 serving glasses to create a fun effect.

Add the ice cream, tahini, the remaining coffee and 12 ice cubes to a blender and blend until smooth. Pour the shake into the serving glasses.

Top with squirty vegan cream, if using, then roughly chop the remaining chocolate and sprinkle it on top. Finish with some coffee beans for decoration.

Tip
You'll be able to find dairy-free squirty cream in vegan food stores, or you can simply order it online.

GRILLED CINNAMON PLUMS

This is the ideal dessert if you're looking for a quick and comforting treat. We absolutely adore plums, especially when they're grilled like this and served with ice cream, which melts all over the soft and juicy fruit. Yum!

Serves 2

3 tbsp maple syrup,
    plus extra for topping
½ tsp ground cinnamon
4 ripe plums
50g walnuts
4 scoops dairy-free
    vanilla ice cream

In a small bowl, combine 1 tablespoon of olive oil, the maple syrup and cinnamon and mix together to create a sweet cinnamon dressing.

Place a griddle pan over a medium heat. Meanwhile, use a sharp knife to halve the plums, then twist each half in the opposite direction to detach them from each other and use a teaspoon to remove the stones. Brush the plum halves with the cinnamon dressing, reserving any leftover dressing for later. Then add the plum halves to the hot griddle pan, cut-side down, and fry for 5 minutes, then turn over and fry for a further 2 minutes, until caramelised.

Meanwhile, roughly chop the walnuts and toast them in a small frying pan over a medium heat for 5 minutes. Stir in the remaining cinnamon dressing and fry for 1 minute.

To serve, divide the grilled plums between 2 shallow bowls, top each portion with a couple of scoops of ice cream, sprinkle the walnuts on top and drizzle with a generous amount of extra maple syrup.

Tips
British plums deserve so much more credit. They have a lovely mellow flavour and you'll find them in supermarkets from late July to early October.

SO VEGAN IN 5

🕐 **Prep** 20 mins, plus chilling/setting   🕐 **Cook** 5 mins   £ £

CHOCOLATE ORANGE BRANDY MOUSSE

Serves 4

4 medium oranges
100g dairy-free dark chocolate,
    plus extra to decorate
300g silken tofu
2 tbsp brandy
3 tbsp maple syrup

Rich, decadent and boozy, this dessert is an absolute delight. The silken tofu creates a creamy mousse-like texture, while dark chocolate pairs perfectly with the orange and brandy.

Slice the tops off the oranges roughly 2cm down and use a spoon to scoop out the flesh over a bowl to create 4 orange shells, catching the juice below to use later. Set aside.

Add the dark chocolate to a heatproof bowl set over a pan of gently simmering water (make sure the bottom of the bowl doesn't come into contact with the water underneath). Stir the chocolate occasionally, until completely melted, then remove the bowl and leave it to one side.

Wrap the tofu inside a clean tea towel, squeezing out as much moisture as possible. Add the tofu to a food processor along with the melted chocolate, brandy, maple syrup and 100ml of the fresh orange juice you collected in the bowl. Use a top from one or two of the oranges to grate ½ teaspoon of zest into the processor. Finally, add a generous pinch of salt, then blend everything together for a minute or two, until it develops a lovely smooth texture.

Spoon the mousse into the orange shells, then transfer to the fridge for 2 hours to set. When they're ready to serve, decorate the mousses with extra grated dark chocolate scattered on top.

Tip
We use the leftover flesh from the oranges for smoothies!

SO VEGAN IN 5

GINGER BISCUITS

Sometimes it's important to appreciate the simple things in life, like dunking a crispy ginger biscuit into a lovely cup of tea. These wonderful little things have that perfect snap, and we usually have a batch on hand whenever friends drop by for a cheeky brew.

Makes 18 biscuits

140g self-raising flour,
    plus extra for dusting
1½ tsp ground ginger
90g dark muscovado sugar
80g dairy-free margarine
1 ball of preserved stem ginger

Add the flour, ground ginger, sugar, margarine and a pinch of salt to a food processor and process until the mixture forms a dough. Roughly chop the stem ginger, add to the food processor, then pulse a few times to combine.

Roll the dough into a ball, wrap it in a sheet of baking paper and refrigerate for 30 minutes.

Preheat the oven to 200°/180°C fan/gas mark 6 and line 2 large baking trays with baking paper.

Generously dust a work surface and a rolling pin with flour, then roll out the dough until it's roughly 5mm thick. Use a 6cm-round cutter to stamp out the biscuits, using up all the dough (and re-rolling it, if necessary) until you have 18 biscuits.

Transfer the biscuits to the lined baking trays, leaving a 3cm gap between each biscuit. Bake in the oven for 12 minutes, until lightly brown.

Remove from the oven and leave the biscuits to cool completely before serving. These biscuits will keep in an airtight container for up to 5 days.

COCONUT BANANA BREAD

Roxy grew up surrounded by the sweet smell of freshly made banana bread in the house and it didn't take her long to master a vegan version of this classic recipe. We wanted to make something extra special for this cookbook, so we turned to coconut for a tasty twist.

Makes 8 slices

400g peeled ripe bananas,
    plus 1 extra ripe banana
4 tbsp coconut oil, melted,
    plus extra for greasing
200g self-raising wholemeal flour
120g golden caster sugar
40g desiccated coconut

Preheat the oven to 200°C/180°C fan/gas mark 6 and line a 450g (approx. 20 x 10cm) loaf tin with coconut oil, then line the loaf tin with baking paper.

Add the peeled bananas to a large mixing bowl and mash with a fork until smooth.

Add the coconut oil, flour, sugar, desiccated coconut, a pinch of salt and 1 teaspoon of apple cider vinegar to the mashed bananas, then stir all the ingredients together until they're fully combined. Pour the mixture evenly into the prepared loaf tin.

Peel, then cut the remaining banana in half lengthways and place both halves on top of the bread mixture for decoration.

Bake in the oven for 45 minutes or until a toothpick or fine skewer comes out clean when inserted into the centre of the bread. If the bread isn't quite ready, return it to the oven for a further 5–10 minutes, then check again.

Once it's ready, remove from the oven and leave the bread to cool in the tin for 10 minutes before turning it out, ready for serving. Serve warm or cold in slices. Any leftover banana bread will keep in an airtight container for up to 5 days in the fridge.

Tip
Ripe bananas are vital for the perfect banana bread; the browner the better!

CLAIRE'S JAM TARTS

Here's another winning entry from our cookbook competition. Claire takes these cute little jam tarts to the next level using marzipan, fresh raspberries and flaked almonds. They're sweet, easy to make and one of our new favourite treats. Thank you, Claire!

Makes 12 tarts

2 x 300g sheets of
    dairy-free puff pastry
150g marzipan
240g raspberry jam
1 tbsp flaked almonds
110g fresh raspberries

Preheat the oven to 200°C/180°C fan/gas mark 6 and lightly grease a 12-hole cupcake tin with olive oil.

Unroll the pastry sheets onto a work surface, then use a round pastry cutter, about 2cm larger than a cupcake hole, to cut out 12 rounds of pastry. Line each cupcake hole in the tin with a pastry round, gently pushing the pastry against the base and sides of the hole, then prick the base of each pastry case a couple of times with a fork.

Roll out the marzipan until it's 2mm thick. Use a smaller pastry cutter than before to cut out 12 rounds of marzipan that will cover the base of the pastry cases. Place the marzipan rounds inside the tart cases, then add roughly 2 teaspoons of jam to each tart. Bake in the oven for about 15 minutes or until the pastry is cooked and golden brown.

Remove from the oven and set the tarts to one side, until the jam stops bubbling, then carefully transfer to a wire rack.

Meanwhile, add the flaked almonds to a frying pan over a medium heat and toast for 3–4 minutes, until golden brown, shaking the pan frequently.

While still warm, add a raspberry or two to each tart and sprinkle over the toasted almond flakes. Leave to cool completely before serving.

Tip
Most shop-bought marzipan is vegan-friendly, but it's always worth double-checking the ingredients to be sure.

SO VEGAN IN 5

RUSTIC TARTE TATIN

How good does this look? We're so chuffed we managed to veganise this classic French dessert using only five ingredients. We love its rustic charm and the combination of traditional flavours, which all come together to create a totally winning pud.

Serves 8

1 x 320g sheet of dairy-free
    shortcrust pastry
6 Golden Delicious apples
100g golden caster sugar
1 vanilla pod
dairy-free vanilla ice
    cream, for serving

Preheat the oven to 220°C/200°C fan/gas mark 7.

Roll out the pastry so it's a few centimetres wider than the 28cm ovenproof frying pan that you'll be using to bake the tarte tatin in, and set it aside for later.

Peel the apples, then remove the cores and cut each apple in half. Set aside.

Pour the sugar into the ovenproof frying pan over a medium heat and shake the pan so the sugar is distributed evenly. Watch closely as the sugar starts to heat up, and give the sugar a stir with a silicone spatula if the middle starts to melt faster than the edges. It should take roughly 2–5 minutes for the sugar to turn an amber brown, at which stage you should remove the pan from the heat.

Halve the vanilla pod lengthways, scrape out the seeds, then add both the pod and seeds to the caramel in the pan, along with a pinch of salt.

Arrange the apple halves, rounded-side down, neatly and tightly on top of the caramel. Cover the pan with the pastry, trim the edges if necessary so the pastry forms a neat circle, then use a couple of wooden spoons to tuck in the pastry edges (don't use your hands because the pan will be really hot!).

Using a knife, poke a few holes in the pastry so the steam can escape from the tart. Bake in the oven for 30 minutes or until the pastry is cooked and golden brown.

Remove from the oven, then carefully invert the tart onto a serving plate or a wooden board. Serve with scoops of dairy-free vanilla ice cream. Yum.

SIDES

Garlic bread swirls

Rosemary & thyme roast potatoes

Harissa-roasted broccoli

Parsley & mint chickpea salad

Asian greens

Smoky chargrilled corn

Olive & rosemary focaccia

Chipotle tomato rice

Za'atar wedges with tahini sauce

Easy peasy rice

Peanut butter slaw

Hoisin-glazed carrots

Tangy potato & dill salad

Roasted Brussels sprouts

GARLIC BREAD SWIRLS

Makes 10 swirls

250g strong white bread flour,
plus extra for dusting
½ tbsp fast-action dried yeast
250g mushrooms
6 garlic cloves
100g dairy-free margarine

These brilliant bread swirls are perfect for sharing with friends, but we won't judge if you decide to eat them all by yourself!

Combine the flour with ½ teaspoon of salt in a large mixing bowl, stir in the yeast, then make a well in the middle. Measure 160ml of tepid water and pour this into the well along with 1 tablespoon of olive oil. Mix the ingredients together, then transfer the dough to a well-floured surface and knead for 10 minutes. Transfer the dough to a lightly oiled bowl, cover with a clean tea towel and leave it to prove somewhere warm for 1 hour or so, until the dough has doubled in size.

Heat a little olive oil in a frying pan over a high heat. Thinly slice the mushrooms, add to the pan and fry for 10 minutes or until they've lost most of their moisture, stirring occasionally.

Peel and finely chop the garlic, then add to a mixing bowl along with the fried mushrooms, vegan margarine and a generous pinch of salt and pepper, and stir. Set the bowl to one side, while you finish preparing the dough.

Punch the dough a few times to remove the air bubbles and transfer it to a well-floured work surface. Flour the rolling pin and roll the dough into a rectangle roughly 30 x 10cm, with one of the longest sides facing you. Trim the edges to create neat straight lines.

Spread the mushroom and garlic filling over the entire surface of the dough, then roll the dough away from you into a log. Create the individual swirls by cutting the log into slices at 2–3cm intervals.

Arrange the swirls in a circle in an ovenproof dish, spaced 1cm apart, and cover with a clean tea towel. Leave to prove for another 20 minutes. Meanwhile, preheat the oven to 220°C/200°C fan/gas mark 7. Bake the swirls in the oven for 20 minutes, until the dough turns a light brown colour.

Remove from the oven and brush the top of the swirls with any melted margarine that has collected in the middle of the dish. If there is no margarine left, simply melt an extra tablespoon of vegan margarine and brush it on top of the swirls. Tuck in.

ROSEMARY & THYME ROAST POTATOES

Serves 4–6

1.2kg Maris Piper potatoes
1 tbsp semolina
3 fresh thick rosemary sprigs
3 fresh thick thyme sprigs
8 garlic cloves

When done right, the humble roast potato is impossible to beat. We absolutely adore them in our home. Crispy on the outside and fluffy on the inside, we use semolina to give these rosemary and thyme roasties that extra crunch.

Peel the potatoes, discarding the skins. Cut the large potatoes in half, then add the potatoes to a large saucepan and cover with cold water. Bring to the boil and boil for 10 minutes.

Drain the potatoes into a colander and leave to cool for 20 minutes. It's important to let them steam to release as much moisture as possible. (Tip: If it's Christmas Day, leave the potatoes outside to cool down even more. The cooler they are when you roast them, the crispier they'll be!)

Meanwhile, preheat the oven to 220°C/200°C fan/gas mark 7.

Return the potatoes to the saucepan and season with 1 teaspoon of salt, 1 teaspoon of pepper, the semolina and 2 tablespoons of olive oil. Cover the pan with a lid or a plate and shake the potatoes so their edges break and they become fluffy. Transfer the potatoes to a roasting tray and roast in the oven for 35 minutes.

Pick the leaves off the rosemary and thyme sprigs, and combine them in a small bowl with ½ tablespoon of olive oil. Peel and roughly chop the garlic cloves, then add to the herby oil.

Remove the potatoes from the oven and pour the herby garlic oil over them, carefully mixing together, then roast for a further 15 minutes, until golden and crispy. Enjoy!

Tip
For crispy potato peel skins, throw the potato peelings into a bowl and toss with a drizzle of olive oil and a pinch of salt. Spread out on a baking tray and roast in the oven until golden, about 20–25 minutes.

HARISSA-ROASTED BROCCOLI

Broccoli has a lot going for it. It's packed with fibre and it's so easy to cook. When we're not steaming it for a low-calorie side, we're roasting it with harissa and topping it with creamy tahini to make a devilish accessory to a homemade feast.

Serves 2–3

2 tsp harissa paste
300g Tenderstem broccoli
1 garlic clove
2 tbsp tahini
1 lemon, plus extra
    wedges to serve

Preheat the oven to 200ºC/180ºC fan/gas mark 6.

In a mixing bowl, combine the harissa paste with 2 tablespoons of olive oil, a generous pinch of salt and pepper and 1 tablespoon of cold water to create a sauce.

Trim any leaves off the broccoli and add the broccoli to the mixing bowl. Stir until the broccoli is fully coated in the harissa sauce.

Transfer the broccoli to a baking tray and bake in the oven for 20 minutes, until tender, turning halfway through so they cook evenly.

Meanwhile, prepare the tahini dressing. Peel and mince the garlic, then add to a small bowl with the tahini, the juice from the lemon, 2 tablespoons of cold water and a pinch of salt and pepper, and stir to combine.

Remove the broccoli from the oven and serve each portion with a generous drizzle of tahini dressing and grate the zest from half of the lemon on top. Serve with lemon wedges.

'There's always some healthy competition

between the two of us over who can create the best So Vegan recipe!'

PARSLEY & MINT CHICKPEA SALAD

The simple combination of mint and parsley is unbeatable; it's fresh, vibrant and it makes for an incredibly versatile salad. This is our stripped-back version of a classic tabbouleh, using the humble chickpea alongside some fresh ingredients to create a quick and easy side.

Serves 4

400g tin chickpeas
large bunch of fresh flat-leaf parsley
large handful of fresh mint leaves
4 ripe tomatoes
1 lemon

Roughly chop the parsley and discard any stalks. Pick and roughly chop the mint leaves. Drain and rinse the chickpeas, then add to a mixing bowl along with both herbs.

Cut the tomatoes into 5mm cubes and add them to the mixing bowl along with their juices.

Prepare the dressing by adding the juice from the lemon to a small bowl along with ½ teaspoon of salt, ¼ teaspoon of pepper and 2 tablespoons of extra virgin olive oil. Stir to mix, then pour over the salad and mix until everything is combined. Enjoy.

Tip
The parsley stalks can be quite bitter, so save them to use in your next homemade stock or soup.

ASIAN GREENS

Years ago we'd have visited a Chinese restaurant and ordered as much meat as we could. Today, you'll find us requesting an array of forgotten veggies, which if done right can be a real joy to eat. Here we keep things simple, showing you how to prepare awesome Asian greens in a matter of minutes.

Serves 2

½ thumb-sized piece of fresh ginger
1 fresh red chilli
1½ tbsp black bean garlic sauce
1 tsp white granulated sugar
300g pak choi

Peel and finely chop the ginger, then add to a small bowl. Thinly slice the red chilli, then add it to the bowl along with the sauce, sugar, 1 tablespoon of apple cider vinegar and 3 tablespoons of cold water, and mix everything together. Set to one side.

Separate the pak choi into individual leaves, trim and discard the ends, then rinse the leaves under cold water to remove any dirt. Heat 1 tablespoon of olive oil in a large skillet or a wok over a high heat. When the oil is hot, add the pak choi leaves and fry for 4 minutes, turning frequently to prevent them from burning.

Stir the sauce into the pak choi and cover the pan with a lid. Reduce the heat to medium and leave to steam-fry for 2 minutes.

Serve the pak choi on a plate, covered in all the remaining sauce from the pan.

Tip
If you enjoy spicy food, leave the seeds in the chilli, otherwise discard them.

SMOKY CHARGRILLED CORN

Serves 4

4 ears/cobs of corn
1 tsp cumin seeds
3 tbsp dairy-free margarine
1 tsp smoked paprika
1 lime

Grilled corn on the cob is always a winner, especially when it's charred to perfection and seasoned beautifully with just the right amount of smoked paprika. We'll often make these at home, or they'll take centre stage at a BBQ with family and friends.

Prepare the corn by discarding the leaves and silks.

Heat a griddle pan over a medium-high heat. Once the pan is hot, add the corn and cook for 30 minutes, turning it every few minutes to make sure the kernels cook evenly and become nicely charred.

Meanwhile, place a small saucepan over a medium heat. As soon as the saucepan is hot, add the cumin seeds and toast for a minute. Add the margarine, ½ teaspoon of the smoked paprika and a pinch of salt and pepper, and stir until the margarine has completely melted, then remove the pan from the heat.

When the corn has finished cooking, brush the buttery sauce evenly over the charred kernels.

Cut the lime into quarters. Squeeze the juice from 1 lime quarter over the corn ears/cobs and sprinkle them with the remaining ½ teaspoon of smoked paprika. Serve on a platter with the remaining wedges of lime.

OLIVE & ROSEMARY FOCACCIA

This is, without doubt, our favourite way to make bread at home. The beauty with this focaccia is you can enjoy it all by itself or, like we often do, use it to soak up delicious pasta sauces. Best served warm, straight out of the oven.

Serves 8

520g strong white bread flour, plus extra for dusting
1 tbsp white caster sugar
1½ tsp fast-action dried yeast
100g mixed fresh olives, pitted
2 fresh rosemary sprigs

Add the flour, sugar, yeast and 1 teaspoon of salt to a large mixing bowl. Mix everything together, then form a well in the middle and add 300ml of tepid water and 3 tablespoons of olive oil. Use a wooden spoon to mix all the ingredients together to make a dough, then transfer the dough to a floured surface and knead it for 10 minutes. If the dough sticks to the surface, simply add pinches of more flour as you go.

Transfer the dough to a lightly oiled bowl, cover with a damp tea towel and leave to rest somewhere warm for at least an hour or until it has doubled in size.

When the dough is ready, use your fists to lightly punch most of the air out. Use a little olive oil to grease a baking tray, about 30 x 20cm in size and 5cm deep. Add the dough to the tray and carefully stretch it out to the corners using your fingers. Cover the tray with the damp tea towel and leave the dough to prove for another 30 minutes.

Meanwhile, preheat the oven to 220ºC/200ºC fan/gas mark 7.

Use your fingers to punch holes in the dough 2–3cm apart and then push the olives to the bottom of the holes. Break up the rosemary sprigs, discarding the tough stalks, then push most of the leaves into the dough, distributing them evenly.

Finely chop the remaining rosemary leaves and add them to a small bowl with 2 teaspoons of olive oil, then use a brush to coat the top of the dough with the rosemary oil, and sprinkle over a little more salt.

Bake in the oven for 18–20 minutes, until the bread is lightly golden on top.

Remove from the oven and cut the focaccia into chunks to serve.

CHIPOTLE TOMATO RICE

We'll rarely let rice simmer away on its own. We're always attempting to turn it into something special by throwing in a host of ingredients pulled out of our kitchen cupboards. This tomato rice is one of our best; it's outrageously moreish and the chipotle delivers a reassuringly spicy kick.

Serves 4

1 onion
4 garlic cloves
200g brown rice
2 tsp chipotle paste
400ml passata

Peel and finely chop the onion and garlic. Add a little olive oil to a saucepan over a medium heat. Once the oil is hot, add the onion and fry for 10 minutes, stirring occasionally. Add the garlic and fry for a further 2 minutes.

Rinse the rice under cold water for roughly 10–15 seconds, then drain and add it to the saucepan. Stir in the chipotle paste and cook for 2 minutes, stirring occasionally, until the rice is lightly toasted.

Add the passata and 350ml of cold water to the rice. Bring to the boil, then cover the pan with a lid and reduce the heat to the lowest setting so the rice steams and doesn't burn at the bottom. Leave the rice to cook for 1 hour and avoid removing the lid to prevent the heat from escaping.

After an hour, check if the rice is cooked. If it's not, add the lid back on and cook for another 5–10 minutes, adding a few extra splashes of water, if necessary.

Once the rice is ready, remove from the heat and season to taste with salt and pepper. Leave the rice to stand with the lid off for 5–10 minutes before serving.

ZA'ATAR WEDGES WITH TAHINI SAUCE

There's a special shop in Finsbury Park, North London, that sells the most amazing naan and flatbreads, which is where we first discovered za'atar. We were like kids tasting ice cream for the first time, and ever since then we've been hooked on this magical spice. Here we combine it with tahini, garlic and lime to flavour these Middle Eastern-inspired crispy wedges.

Serves 4

600g baking potatoes
2 tbsp za'atar
4 garlic cloves (skin on)
80g tahini
1 lime

Preheat the oven to 220ºC/200ºC fan/gas mark 7 and line a large baking tray with baking paper.

Rinse and pat dry the potatoes, then slice them in half, then into quarters and finally into eighths so you're left with evenly sized wedges. Drain and rinse the wedges under cold water to remove any excess starch, then leave them on a kitchen towel to dry for a few minutes. When they're dry, add them to a mixing bowl along with the za'atar, 1 tablespoon of olive oil and ½ teaspoon of salt. Mix everything together until the wedges are fully coated in the seasoning.

Place the potato wedges, skin-side down, on the lined baking tray. Brush any remaining seasoning over the wedges. Roast in the oven for 25 minutes.

Remove the tray from the oven. Add the garlic cloves and roast for a further 20–25 minutes, until the wedges are golden all over and dark around the edges.

Tip
Tahini can vary a lot in quality, so it's well worth investing a little extra in one that's organic. You'll totally notice the difference in the richer taste and smoother texture.

Remove the tray from the oven. Take off the skin from the garlic and add the cloves to a blender along with the tahini, the juice from the lime, a pinch of salt and 100ml of cold water. Blend everything together. The tahini sauce should be thick but runny. Add more water if required and blend until the sauce reaches the right consistency.

Pile the wedges on top of each other in the middle of a plate. Pour over half the tahini sauce and grate the zest from the lime over the top. Serve alongside the remaining tahini sauce for dipping!

EASY PEASY RICE

This one-pot rice is creamy and fragrant, and it couldn't be any easier. It's inspired by the traditional Jamaican rice and peas, a dish Ben learned to master while he was at university.

Serves 6

200g basmati rice
400g tin kidney beans
400ml tin coconut milk
1 tsp ground all-spice
2 fresh thyme sprigs

Rinse the rice in a sieve until the water runs clear, then transfer it to a large saucepan. Drain and rinse the kidney beans, then add to the saucepan along with the coconut milk, all-spice and a generous pinch of salt and pepper. Strip the leaves off the thyme sprigs, roughly chop them and add to the saucepan.

Pour 250ml of cold water into the saucepan, stir everything together and bring the rice to the boil, then reduce the heat to the lowest setting, cover the pan with a lid and simmer for 20–25 minutes or until the rice is tender.

Once the rice is ready, remove from the heat and season to taste with extra salt and pepper, if required. Leave the rice to stand with the lid off for 5–10 minutes before serving.

PEANUT BUTTER SLAW

A tasty coleslaw like this one will always come in handy. You can serve it with burgers, tacos and grilled veggies, or practically anything that's cooked on a BBQ. It took us a while to get this just right, that was until we tried it with our favourite crunchy peanut butter, and the rest is history.

Serves 4

100g celeriac
100g red cabbage
1 medium carrot
½ thumb-sized piece of fresh ginger
2 tbsp crunchy peanut butter

Peel the celeriac and trim the ends off the carrot. Use some nifty knife skills, ideally with the help of a mandoline, to julienne the celeriac, cabbage and carrot, then transfer everything to a salad bowl.

Peel and finely chop the ginger. Add the ginger to a small bowl along with the peanut butter, 1 tablespoon of apple cider vinegar, 3 tablespoons of extra virgin olive oil, 2 tablespoons of cold water and a generous pinch of salt and pepper. Use a spoon to mix everything together until smooth.

Pour the peanut butter dressing over the slaw and use your hands to mix everything together.

Top with some extra grinds of pepper to serve.

HOISIN-GLAZED CARROTS

Hoisin and orange is a totally winning combo, it's sweet and sticky, but fresh and zesty at the same time. We always top these carrots with a generous helping of crunchy spring onions, served alongside our favourite Chinese-inspired dishes.

Serves 4

500g carrots
2½ tbsp hoisin sauce
½ orange
½ tbsp sesame seeds
2 spring onions

Scrub the carrots (the skin contains lots of nutrients and flavour so we always leave it on), remove any stalks and slice the carrots in half.

Heat a little olive oil in a large pan over a low-medium heat. Once hot, add the carrots, hoisin sauce, 1 ½ tablespoons of juice from the orange half and a pinch of salt and pepper. Mix everything together and cook with the lid on for 15 minutes.

Remove the lid and cook the carrots for a further 2–3 minutes to reduce the sauce.

Take the pan off the heat, add the sesame seeds and any remaining juice from the orange half, then stir everything together.

Trim the ends and thinly slice the spring onions. Scatter the sliced spring onions on top of the glazed carrots and grate the zest from the orange half over the top, then serve.

Tip
Nowadays, you can find tasty and authentic hoisin sauce in most major supermarkets, usually in the world foods aisle.

TANGY POTATO & DILL SALAD

Forget what you know about potato salads. Our twist on this traditional summer dish is healthier and lighter. We'll find any excuse to use dill and it works so well here with the tangy mustard and caramelised shallots. This will be your new favourite way to enjoy the humble potato.

Serves 4

750g new potatoes
2 shallots
2 tsp Dijon mustard
140g radishes
large handful of fresh dill

Cut any large potatoes in half. Add all the potatoes to a saucepan and cover with cold water. Bring the water to the boil and cook for 15 minutes or until the potatoes are soft.

Meanwhile, heat a little olive oil in a frying pan on a medium heat. While the oil is heating up, peel and finely slice the shallots then add them to the frying pan and fry for 6 mins or until caramelised.

Prepare the dressing by adding the mustard to a small mixing bowl along with 2 tablespoons of extra virgin olive oil, 1 tablespoon of apple cider vinegar, ½ teaspoon of salt and ½ teaspoon of pepper. Stir to combine then set to one side.

Drain the potatoes and leave them to cool. Add the potatoes to a large serving bowl and lightly crush them with a fork to help soak up the dressing. Trim the ends off the radishes, then slice them thinly using a sharp knife or a mandoline. Add them to the serving bowl along with the fried shallots and salad dressing.

Roughly chop the dill and add it to the serving bowl. Stir everything together and serve.

TIP

Not all Dijon mustard brands
are vegan because some contain
white wine vinegar. But a quick
search online will tell you which
brands are good to go.

🕐 **Prep** 15 mins   🕐 **Cook** 25 mins   £

ROASTED BRUSSELS SPROUTS

Brussels sprouts get a bad rep, but as far as we're concerned they're one of the highlights of the festive season. The trick is cooking them just long enough so the skins char and caramelise. We throw radishes into the mix for their gorgeous pink colour, and use agave to sweeten the entire dish. Lovely.

Serves 4

350g Brussels sprouts
200g radishes
½ onion
½ lemon
2 tsp agave syrup

Preheat the oven to 220°C/200°C fan/gas mark 7.

Trim and halve the Brussels sprouts, then transfer to a baking tray. Drizzle with a splash of olive oil, season with a pinch of salt and pepper and combine with your hands. Bake in the oven for 10 minutes.

Trim and halve the radishes, then add to the baking tray of sprouts and bake them together for a further 15 minutes or until the sprouts are nicely charred.

Meanwhile, heat a drizzle of olive oil in a frying pan over a medium heat. Thinly slice the onion, add to the pan and fry for 20 minutes, stirring frequently, until crispy.

Prepare the dressing by combining the juice from the lemon with the agave syrup in a small bowl.

Transfer the roasted sprouts and radishes to a serving plate. Top with the crispy onion slices, then drizzle over the lemon and agave dressing to finish.

DIPS & SNACKS

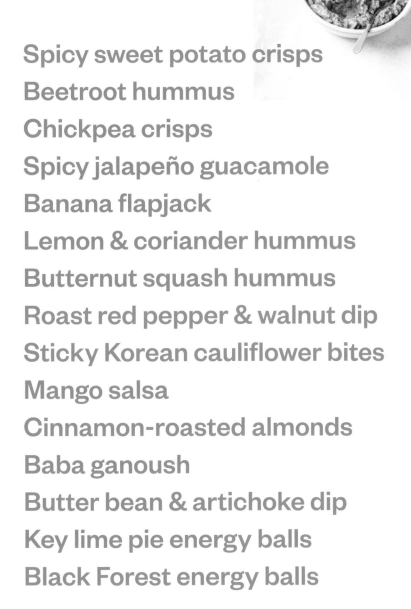

Spicy sweet potato crisps

Beetroot hummus

Chickpea crisps

Spicy jalapeño guacamole

Banana flapjack

Lemon & coriander hummus

Butternut squash hummus

Roast red pepper & walnut dip

Sticky Korean cauliflower bites

Mango salsa

Cinnamon-roasted almonds

Baba ganoush

Butter bean & artichoke dip

Key lime pie energy balls

Black Forest energy balls

SPICY SWEET POTATO CRISPS

This is inspired by one of the most popular So Vegan recipes ever, our homemade vegetable crisps. They're a welcome snack if you're looking for a healthier and far tastier alternative to the crisps you'll find at your local newsagents!

Serves 1, generously

1 sweet potato (about 180g)
generous pinch of chilli powder
½ tsp garlic powder
½ tsp smoked paprika
½ tsp ground cumin

Preheat the oven to 160°C/140°C fan/gas mark 3 and line a large baking tray with baking paper.

Trim the ends off the sweet potato. Use a sharp knife or mandoline to thinly slice the sweet potato (approx. 2mm thick), then add the slices to a mixing bowl.

Add the chilli powder, garlic powder, smoked paprika, ¼ teaspoon of salt, ¼ teaspoon of pepper and 1 tablespoon of olive oil to a small bowl and stir to combine. Pour the seasoning over the sweet potato slices and use your hands to make sure all of the slices are fully coated.

Transfer the sweet potato slices to the lined baking tray, making sure they're a single layer and not touching each other. Bake in the oven for 40–50 minutes or until crisp.

Remove from the oven and leave the potato crisps to cool completely on the baking tray before serving.

BEETROOT HUMMUS

We love beetroot for its earthy flavour, vibrant colour and the fact that it turns practically everything purple. The parsley and lemon bring this dish to life, balancing perfectly with the beetroot, while the creamy chickpeas and tahini do the rest.

Makes 1 pot

300g raw beetroot
400g tin chickpeas
50g tahini
1 lemon
large handful of fresh flat-leaf parsley, plus extra to garnish

Preheat the oven to 220ºC/200ºC fan/gas mark 7 and line a baking tray with baking paper.

Trim the ends off the beetroot, then peel them, discarding the skins. Slice into 1cm cubes and transfer to the lined baking tray. Drizzle with olive oil and a sprinkling of salt and pepper. Cook in the oven for 30 minutes, until tender, then remove from the oven and leave to cool.

Drain and rinse the chickpeas, then transfer them to a food processor along with the tahini, beetroot, juice and zest from the lemon, parsley, 1 tablespoon of extra virgin olive oil and 4 tablespoons of cold water. Blend until smooth, then season to taste with salt and pepper.

Serve the hummus in a small bowl with a drizzle of extra virgin olive oil and a few leaves of fresh parsley on top.

CHICKPEA CRISPS

This is our healthy alternative to buying salty snacks. We'll often experiment with different herb and spice combinations, but here's our tried-and-tested seasoning for a quick, easy and guilt-free snack.

Serves 2 as a snack

400g tin chickpeas
1 tsp garlic powder
1 tsp ground cumin
1 tsp paprika
small handful of fresh coriander

Preheat the oven to 220°C/200°C fan/gas mark 7 and line a baking tray with baking paper.

Drain, rinse and pat dry the chickpeas, discarding any skins that come off. Place the chickpeas in a small bowl and toss in 1 tablespoon of olive oil and a generous pinch of salt.

Transfer the chickpeas to the lined baking tray, spreading them out in an even layer, then bake in the oven for 35–40 minutes. Turn the tray around halfway through (often the temperature will vary closest to the oven door), while keeping an eye on the chickpeas so that they don't burn.

Remove from the oven and carefully transfer the chickpeas to a small bowl. Toss them in the garlic powder, cumin, paprika and a pinch of pepper. Be careful as they will still be hot. Leave to cool completely. The chickpeas will crisp up as they cool.

Finely chop the coriander and stir into the chickpeas to serve.

'So Vegan has been a truly unforgettable journey, and we couldn't have done it without everyone's support.'

SPICY JALAPEÑO GUACAMOLE

Fresh jalapeños make all the difference here. They're one of the tastiest chillies that money can buy and they'll easily turn an average guacamole into a truly spectacular dip. If you can't find them fresh, you can always use a more common variety of chilli. But make sure you keep it fresh!

Makes 1 pot

2 ripe avocados
1 lime
1 fresh green jalapeño pepper
½ small red onion
small handful of fresh coriander

Halve the avocados and remove the stones. Scoop the flesh into a small mixing bowl, then add the juice from the lime and a splash of extra virgin olive oil. Use a fork to mash the avocado flesh until smooth.

Cut the jalapeño in half and discard the seeds. Finely chop the jalapeño and red onion, roughly chop the coriander, then add them to the mashed avocado. Season with salt and pepper to taste and stir until everything is combined, then serve.

Tip
It's surprisingly easy to grow chillies in the UK, so consider hanging onto those seeds! Sow the seeds indoors until around mid-spring, before moving the plants to a sunny spot outdoors. Remember to water them regularly and feed occasionally.

BANANA FLAPJACK

These are the ideal pre- or post-workout treat. The combination of oats, nuts and seeds mean these flapjacks provide you with slow-releasing energy, keeping you fuller for longer. Not to mention those bananas, which are pretty good for you, too.

Makes 9 squares

3 ripe bananas
100g mixed nuts and seeds
200g jumbo oats
4 tbsp maple syrup
1 tbsp coconut oil, melted

Preheat the oven to 200°C/180°C fan/gas mark 6 and line a 20 x 20cm square baking tin with baking paper.

Peel the bananas and transfer them to a mixing bowl. Mash them until they become runny and no lumps remain.

Roughly chop the nuts and seeds, then add them to the mixing bowl along with the remaining ingredients and mix well.

Pour the mixture into the prepared baking tin and use the back of a spoon to push the mixture down so it's level and compact. Bake in the oven for 30 minutes or until golden brown.

Remove from the oven and leave to cool in the tin for 15 minutes. Remove the flapjack from the tin by pulling it out using the baking paper, and transfer to a wire rack. Leave to cool completely before slicing into 9 squares. Store any leftovers in an airtight container for up to 7 days.

LEMON & CORIANDER HUMMUS

Makes 1 pot

400g tin chickpeas
1 garlic clove
1 lemon
70g tahini
small handful of fresh coriander,
    plus extra to garnish

Hummus is like gold dust in our home. It never lasts long and you'll occasionally find us squabbling over who is owed the last mouthful! Aside from it tasting so much better, one of the best things about making your own is you can adjust the ingredients to suit your taste.

Drain and rinse the chickpeas, then set half a dozen or so chickpeas to one side to use later for the garnish.

Peel the garlic and add to a food processor along with the juice of the lemon, the zest of half the lemon, tahini, coriander, 2 tablespoons of extra virgin olive oil, 1 teaspoon of salt, ½ teaspoon of pepper and 4 tablespoons of cold water, and blend until smooth.

Transfer to a small bowl, garnish with the reserved chickpeas and a sprinkling of chopped coriander and serve with a light drizzle of extra virgin olive oil.

Tip
You can save money by buying raw/dry chickpeas, soaking them overnight and then cooking them yourself, instead of using tinned chickpeas.

BUTTERNUT SQUASH HUMMUS

Mix things up with this smoky twist on hummus. Baharat is a Middle Eastern spice blend, adding warmth and depth, and it pairs really well with butternut squash. You'll be able to find it in the herb and spice section at most supermarkets.

Makes 1 pot

500g butternut squash
2 tsp baharat, plus extra for serving
2 garlic cloves (skin on)
400g tin chickpeas
50g tahini

Preheat the oven to 220°C/200°C fan/gas mark 7 and line a baking tray with baking paper.

Peel the butternut squash and remove the seeds, then cut the flesh into 2cm cubes and transfer to a mixing bowl. Drizzle with some olive oil, add a pinch of salt and pepper and 1½ teaspoons of the baharat. Mix to combine, then transfer to the lined baking tray. Roast in the oven for 20 minutes or until tender.

Remove from the oven, add the garlic cloves to the butternut squash and roast for a further 10 minutes. Remove from the oven and leave everything to cool.

Drain and rinse the chickpeas, then transfer them to a food processor along with the tahini, the remaining ½ teaspoon of baharat, 1 tablespoon of extra virgin olive oil and 4 tablespoons of cold water.

Once the garlic has cooled, remove the skin and add the flesh to the processor along with the butternut squash cubes. Blend until smooth, then season to taste with salt and pepper.

Serve the hummus in a small bowl with a drizzle of extra virgin olive oil and an extra sprinkling of baharat on top.

ROAST RED PEPPER & WALNUT DIP

Makes 1 pot

3 red peppers
80g walnuts
1 tsp cumin seeds
1 tsp maple syrup
1 lemon

This is loosely inspired by the traditional Middle Eastern dip muhammara. We've made a few tweaks, simplifying things but holding onto as much of that amazingly tangy flavour as possible.

Preheat the oven to 250°C/230°C fan/gas mark 10 and line a baking tray with baking paper.

Place the whole peppers on the baking tray and roast them in the oven for 30 minutes or until most of the skins have turned black. Remove from the oven and wrap the peppers in foil, then leave them to steam for 10 minutes. Discard the foil and leave the peppers until they are cool enough to handle.

Meanwhile, place a small frying pan over a medium-high heat. When the pan is hot, add the walnuts and toast for 2 minutes, shaking the pan frequently to prevent the nuts from burning. Add the cumin seeds and toast for a further 1 minute. You want to catch them just as they begin to smoke. Remove from the heat.

Use your hands to discard the stems and remove the skins from the peppers, then use a spoon to remove any seeds. Drain off any excess liquid, then add the peppers to a food processor along with the walnuts (save at least 1 walnut for topping later) and cumin seeds, maple syrup, the juice from the lemon, 2 tablespoons of extra virgin olive oil, ½ teaspoon of salt and ½ teaspoon of pepper. Process for 30 seconds or so, until the mixture is smooth and combined.

Transfer the dip to a small bowl. Roughly chop the remaining walnut and sprinkle it on top along with a drizzle of extra virgin olive oil and a few more grinds of pepper.

Tip
To speed things up, you can use 200g of pre-roasted red peppers straight from a jar, if you like, but we prefer roasting the peppers ourselves because we think it gives the dip more depth of flavour.

STICKY KOREAN CAULIFLOWER BITES

Be warned... these spicy little things have a real kick to them and they're outrageously moreish. For whatever reason, the spicier the food is, the faster we want to eat it. Gochujang (red chilli paste) is very intense and can be quite sour, but the sugar and tamari help to balance everything out.

Serves 4

1 medium cauliflower
80g plain flour
3 tbsp gochujang sauce
2 tbsp caster sugar
2 tbsp tamari (or soy sauce)

Preheat the oven to 220°C/200°C fan/gas mark 7 and line a large baking tray with baking paper.

Remove and discard any green leaves from the cauliflower, then use a sharp knife to cut it into bite-sized florets, discarding any of the long stems as you go.

Add the flour to a large mixing bowl, then pour in 120ml of cold water and stir to combine into a smooth batter. Gently fold the cauliflower florets into the batter until fully coated.

Transfer one floret at a time to the lined baking tray, shaking off any excess batter as you go. Bake in the oven for 15 minutes.

Meanwhile, combine the gochujang sauce, sugar and tamari in a mixing bowl.

Remove the cauliflower florets from the oven. Use a spoon to drop a few of the florets into the gochujang sauce at a time, coating them completely. Return the coated florets to the baking tray and bake in the oven for a further 10–15 minutes, until tender.

Serve immediately.

Tip
You'll find gochujang sauce in the world foods aisle in most big supermarkets, or you can pick it up at a local Asian supermarket like we do.

SO VEGAN IN 5

MANGO SALSA

Mangoes are literally the best, and their sweet, tropical flavour really brings this salsa to life. This is more than just a dip. We'll happily add it to wraps and tacos, or simply serve it as a side at one of our Mexican feasts.

Makes 1 bowl

1 ripe mango
½ red onion
1 red pepper
large handful of fresh coriander
juice of 1 lime

Peel the mango, cut the flesh off around the stone and cut it into 1cm cubes.

Peel and finely slice the onion, then add to a mixing bowl along with the mango. Then dice the red pepper, discarding the seeds, and roughly chop the coriander. Add both to the mixing bowl.

Squeeze the juice from the lime into the bowl, then add a generous pinch of salt and pepper. Stir to combine, then serve.

CINNAMON-ROASTED ALMONDS

Being vegan has turned us into snackaholics. Most of the time we'll turn to fruit, nuts and other healthy ways to boost our energy. But occasionally we'll need something a little sweeter, which is when we'll get these brilliant roasted almonds on the go. They rarely last long in our home!

Makes 1 batch

120g raw whole almonds
1 tbsp coconut oil
¼ tsp vanilla extract
1 tsp ground cinnamon
1½ tbsp soft light brown sugar

Preheat the oven to 200°C/180°C fan/gas mark 6.

Transfer the almonds to a baking tray and roast in the oven for 15 minutes.

Once the almonds are ready, remove from the oven. Add the coconut oil, vanilla extract, ½ teaspoon of the cinnamon and 1 tablespoon of cold water to a small saucepan. Bring the mixture to a gentle simmer, then add the almonds. Fry for 2 minutes or until the water has evaporated, stirring frequently.

Place the remaining cinnamon, the sugar and a pinch of salt in a mixing bowl. Throw in the almonds and toss until they are fully coated.

Transfer the almonds to a serving bowl and leave them to cool a little before serving.

BABA GANOUSH

Aubergine can be divisive. Usually you love it or hate it; there's rarely an in between. But if there's one dish that'll tempt you 'auber' to the dark side, it'll be this brilliant baba ganoush. It's fragrant and smoky, and it's perfect alongside some toasted flatbread.

Makes 1 pot

3 aubergines
1¼ tsp cumin seeds
2 garlic cloves
½ lemon
2 tbsp tahini

Preheat the grill to a medium-high heat.

Prick the aubergines a few times with a fork and place on a baking tray.

Place under the grill for 30 minutes, turning the aubergines every 5 minutes, so that the skins get nice and charred.

Meanwhile, heat a small frying pan over a medium-high heat. Once the pan is hot, add the cumin seeds and toast for 2–3 minutes, making sure you shake the pan frequently to prevent the seeds from burning. Remove from the heat, add 1 teaspoon of the seeds to a food processor, and save the remaining ¼ teaspoon for garnish.

Remove the aubergines from the grill and leave until they're cool enough to handle. Trim and discard the green tops, then peel the aubergines and add the flesh to a sieve set over a bowl. Use a fork to squeeze the aubergine flesh and remove as much liquid as possible, then leave it to sit in the sieve for a further 10 minutes. Press the aubergine flesh against the sieve one more time, then add it to the food processor.

Peel the garlic and add the cloves to the processor along with the juice from the lemon, tahini, 1 tablespoon of extra virgin olive oil and a generous pinch of salt and pepper. Blend until smooth.

Transfer the mixture to a small serving bowl, drizzle with a little extra virgin olive oil and scatter the reserved cumin seeds on top to finish. Get dipping and enjoy.

Tip
You can also char the aubergines using a griddle pan, or better still, you can (carefully) cook them on an open flame if you have a gas hob.

BUTTER BEAN & ARTICHOKE DIP

As much as we're constantly craving hummus in our house, it's always refreshing to try something a bit different. This awesome butter bean and artichoke dip has no problem competing for the pride of place on our dinner table. It's soft and creamy and the thyme gives the dip a wonderfully aromatic flavour.

Makes 1 pot

400g tin butter beans
60g artichokes in oil (from a jar)
1 large fresh thyme sprig
1 garlic clove
1 tbsp lemon juice

Drain and rinse the butter beans, then add to a food processor along with the artichokes, 5 tablespoons of oil from the jar of artichokes and 1 tablespoon of cold water.

Pick the thyme leaves off the sprig and add most of the leaves to the processor (saving a few for the garnish). Peel the garlic and add it to the food processor along with the lemon juice and a generous pinch of salt and pepper.

Blend the butter bean mixture until smooth and combined, then taste and adjust the seasoning, if needed.

Spoon the dip into a bowl and serve with a drizzle of extra virgin olive oil on top, garnished with the reserved thyme leaves.

KEY LIME PIE ENERGY BALLS

This is our healthy spin on the classic key lime pie. The mix of cashews and desiccated coconut creates a creamy consistency, while the lime adds that all-essential zing.

Makes 8 balls

80g Medjool dates
120g raw cashews
70g desiccated coconut
2 limes
1 tbsp coconut oil, melted

Remove and discard the stones from the dates, and add the dates to a food processor along with the cashews, 50g of the desiccated coconut, the zest of 1 lime, the juice from both limes, coconut oil and a pinch of salt. Process until all the ingredients have broken down and the mixture forms a ball.

Divide the mixture into 8 even portions and use your hands to roll each piece into a ball. Place the remaining 20g of desiccated coconut on a small plate and roll each energy ball in the coconut to coat.

Transfer the energy balls to a plate and refrigerate for at least 10 minutes before serving.

BLACK FOREST ENERGY BALLS

These yummy balls are gooey and sweet, and they're a great way to keep those energy levels up. Perfect for an on-the-go snack, we'll keep a few of these in our bags whenever we're out and about, just in case we become stranded and we can't find any vegan food!

Makes 10 balls

120g Medjool dates
3 tbsp cocoa powder
150g raw almonds
2 tbsp coconut oil, melted
100g dried cherries

Remove and discard the stones from the dates, and add the dates to a food processor along with the cocoa powder, almonds, coconut oil and a pinch of salt. Process until all the ingredients have broken down.

Add the dried cherries to the processor and pulse the mixture a few times until the cherries break down into smaller pieces, but avoid processing them completely.

Divide the mixture into 10 even portions and then use your hands to mould each piece into a compact ball. Place the energy balls on a plate and refrigerate for at least 10 minutes before serving.

Tip
Medjool dates can be quite expensive. You can substitute for cheaper dates, but they won't be as sweet.

STAPLES

Almond milk

Chocolate & hazelnut spread

Chive sour cream

Homemade ketchup

Green pesto

Sun-dried tomato pesto

Chipotle mayo

Cashew parmesan cheese

Oat milk

Garlic & thyme cream cheese

Double berry chia jam

Prep 15 mins, plus soaking

Cook no cooking

£

ALMOND MILK

The best thing about making your own plant-based milk is it's far creamier and you can throw in whatever ingredients you like, creating your own unique twists. Here we add tahini for its nutty flavour, Medjool dates for their sweetness and a Brazil nut for extra nutrition.

Makes 700ml milk

2 Medjool dates
3 tbsp almond butter
1 tbsp tahini
½ tsp vanilla extract
1 Brazil nut

Remove and discard the stones from the dates, and add the dates to a blender along with the remaining ingredients, 750ml cold water and a pinch of salt. Leave them to soak for 10 minutes.

Blend all the ingredients together for roughly 2 minutes, until smooth.

Balance a sieve on top of a mixing bowl and place a piece of cheesecloth (or muslin) on top. Pour the blended mixture into the cheesecloth, then pick up the edges to close the cheesecloth tightly. Squeeze the pulp inside the cheesecloth until no more liquid comes out and all the almond milk is left in the mixing bowl underneath.

Transfer the milk to an airtight container and keep it in the fridge for up to a week. Always shake well before using.

Tip
You don't have to use cheesecloth (or muslin). The milk won't be as smooth, but it'll still taste lovely and it'll maintain a creamy consistency.

CHOCOLATE & HAZELNUT SPREAD

Makes 1 jar

150g hazelnuts
3 tbsp golden syrup
1 tsp vanilla extract
1 tbsp cocoa powder
60g dairy-free dark chocolate

Classic food combos don't get much better than chocolate and hazelnut. They belong together, just like Kim and Kanye. You can spread this on toast, add to a porridge, enjoy it with fresh fruit... or simply eat it straight out of the jar like we do.

Preheat the oven to 200°C/180°C fan/gas mark 6.

Transfer the hazelnuts to a baking tray and roast them in the oven for 10 minutes.

Pour the roasted hazelnuts onto a clean tea towel and rub in the towel until the skins come off. Peel any remaining skins off with your fingers.

Add the peeled hazelnuts to a food processor along with the golden syrup, vanilla extract, cocoa powder, a pinch of salt and 1 tablespoon of olive oil. Process for about 5 minutes, until the mixture turns into a nut butter, scraping down the sides as you go. Set to one side.

Add the dark chocolate to a heatproof bowl set over a pan of gently simmering water (make sure the bottom of the bowl doesn't come into contact with the water underneath). Stir the chocolate occasionally, until completely melted, then remove the bowl from the heat and stir in the nut butter mixture until combined.

Transfer the spread to an airtight container and store at room temperature for up to 3 weeks.

Prep 5 mins, plus 10 mins soaking

Cook no cooking

£

CHIVE SOUR CREAM

We'll pair this with almost anything. It's soft, creamy, zesty and amazingly versatile, and you can serve it with burgers and kebabs, breakfasts and brunches or simply homemade snacks. Oh, and it'll take you practically no time at all to make it.

Makes 250ml

120g raw cashews
½ lemon
½ tbsp nutritional yeast
120ml soya milk
large handful of fresh chives

Put the cashews in a small bowl, cover them in hot water from the kettle and leave to soak for 10 minutes.

Drain the cashews and add them to a food processor along with the juice from the lemon, nutritional yeast, soya milk, 1 teaspoon of apple cider vinegar and ½ teaspoon of salt. Process until smooth, scraping down the sides as you go, then remove the blade.

Finely chop the chives (you should be left with roughly 4 tablespoons) and stir them in to the food processor with the sour cream.

Transfer the sour cream to an airtight container and store in the fridge for up to 3–4 days.

HOMEMADE KETCHUP

Give this homemade ketchup a go and you'll never want to buy it ready-made ever again. We rely on the richness from the purée to do most of the work, balancing it with some sugar and our favourite seasonings. Just go easy on the all-spice, because too much will completely overpower the sauce!

Makes 1 small jar

200g tomato purée
2 tbsp light brown
    muscovado sugar
¼ tsp garlic powder
pinch of ground all-spice
¼ tsp smoked paprika

Add all the ingredients to a small saucepan along with 1 tablespoon of apple cider vinegar, ½ teaspoon of salt, ¼ teaspoon of pepper and 50ml of cold water, then cook over a low heat for 15 minutes, stirring occasionally. If the sauce begins to spit, that means the heat is too high, so lower the temperature accordingly.

Remove from the heat and leave the ketchup to cool completely, then transfer it to an airtight container and store in the fridge for up to 2 weeks.

Tip
Have fun experimenting with different seasonings to create your own twists!

GREEN PESTO

This awesome pesto just never gets boring. It's quick and easy to make, and you can combine it with pastas, pizzas, salads, soups and so much more. We prefer to roast the garlic, which reduces any unwanted bitterness and leaves a more aromatic sweet flavour.

Makes over 100g pesto

4 garlic cloves (skin on)
3 tbsp pine nuts
2 tbsp lemon juice
3 tbsp nutritional yeast
70g fresh basil leaves

Preheat the oven to 200°C/180°C fan/gas mark 6.

Place the garlic cloves on a baking tray. Drizzle them with a small splash of olive oil and roast in the oven for 10 minutes. Remove from the oven and leave the garlic to cool for 10 minutes.

Peel the garlic and add the flesh to a food processor along with the pine nuts, lemon juice, nutritional yeast, 2 tablespoons of extra virgin olive oil, ½ teaspoon of salt, ½ teaspoon of pepper and 2 tablespoons of cold water. Add the basil leaves to the food processor and process until smooth and combined.

Transfer the pesto to an airtight container and store in the fridge for up to 1 week.

Tip
Pine nuts can be quite pricey, especially if you're buying them in small quantities. Sub walnuts for a more affordable twist.

Prep 10 mins, plus cooling **Cook** 10 mins £

SUN-DRIED TOMATO PESTO

Somehow it just didn't feel right sharing only one pesto recipe. Here's a classic twist using sun-dried tomatoes, which is another favourite of ours and it's just as easy to make. The tomatoes give the sauce a lovely intense flavour and a subtle sweetness.

Makes over 100g pesto

4 garlic cloves (skin on)
large handful of fresh basil leaves
60g sun-dried tomatoes
3 tbsp pine nuts
2 tbsp nutritional yeast

Preheat the oven to 200°C/180°C fan/gas mark 6.

Place the garlic cloves on a baking tray. Drizzle them with a small splash of olive oil and roast in the oven for 10 minutes. Remove from the oven and leave the garlic to cool for 10 minutes.

Peel the garlic and add the flesh to a food processor along with the basil, sun-dried tomatoes, pine nuts, nutritional yeast, 3 tablespoons of extra virgin olive oil, 1 teaspoon of apple cider vinegar, ½ teaspoon of salt, ½ teaspoon of pepper and 4 tablespoons of cold water. Process until smooth and combined.

Transfer the pesto to an airtight container and store in the fridge for up to 1 week.

TIP

You can easily put your own twist on this pesto recipe. Try walnuts instead of pine nuts for a cheaper alternative, or even avocado instead of sun-dried tomatoes for a creamier texture.

CHIPOTLE MAYO

This is a far healthier and lighter mayo compared to most vegan versions. We use less oil and instead rely on tofu to deliver that soft, creamy texture. There's a generous kick to this mayo, but you can dial the heat up or down, depending on how spicy you like it.

Makes 300ml

350g soft silken tofu
1½ tsp chipotle paste
1½ tbsp lemon juice
½ tsp English mustard
4 tbsp vegetable oil

Add the tofu, chipotle paste, lemon juice, English mustard, 1 teaspoon of salt and ½ teaspoon of pepper to a food processor. Process until smooth.

With the processor running, slowly and gradually pour the vegetable oil through the top (feeder tube) of the food processor, until you have mayo with a smooth, creamy consistency. Scrape down the sides of the processor as you go.

Transfer the chipotle mayo to an airtight container and store in the fridge for up to a week.

🕐 **Prep** 5 mins   🕐 **Cook** no cooking   £

CASHEW PARMESAN CHEESE

Makes 1 small jar

70g raw cashews
2 tbsp nutritional yeast
¼ tsp onion powder
¼ tsp garlic powder
¼ tsp mustard powder

We've been hooked on nutritional yeast ever since we first tried the stuff. It has a nutty and slightly cheesy flavour, and nowadays we'll add it to almost anything, including this outrageously easy cashew parmesan cheese. Simply blend the ingredients together and sprinkle it over your favourite meals.

Add all the ingredients to a small blender or food processor along with ½ teaspoon of salt and process until finely chopped. Depending on the size of your blender or processor, you might need to double the quantities for all the ingredients to break down.

Transfer the cashew parmesan cheese to an airtight container and store in the fridge for up to 2 weeks.

OAT MILK

We always have a supply of oats ready to go. We've come to realise how amazingly versatile they are; we'll use them in smoothies, energy bars, cakes and, of course, oat milk. We'll also fortify the milk with sunflower seeds and a Brazil nut for added nutrition.

Makes 700ml milk

2 Medjool dates
90g rolled oats
2 tbsp sunflower seeds
1 Brazil nut
½ tsp vanilla extract

Remove and discard the stones from the dates, and add them to a blender along with the remaining ingredients, 750ml cold water and a pinch of salt. Leave them to soak for 10 minutes.

Blend all the ingredients together for roughly 2 minutes, until smooth.

Balance a sieve on top of a mixing bowl and place a piece of cheesecloth (or muslin) on top. Pour the blended mixture into the cheesecloth, then pick up the edges to close the cheesecloth tightly. Squeeze the pulp inside the cheesecloth until no more liquid comes out and all the oat milk is left in the mixing bowl underneath.

Transfer the milk to an airtight container and keep it in the fridge for up to a week. Always shake well before using.

Tip
You don't have to use cheesecloth (or muslin). The milk won't be as smooth, but it'll still taste lovely and it'll maintain a creamy consistency.

GARLIC & THYME CREAM CHEESE

Vegan cheese recipes can often be very fiddly and time-consuming, but not this one. We use cashews for their creamy texture and we've made it as easy as possible for you to make at home. Great on crackers and toast, or do what we do and add it as another tasty layer to a sandwich.

Makes 1 pot

250g raw cashews
2 garlic cloves
1 tbsp lemon juice
½ tbsp nutritional yeast
2 fresh thyme sprigs

Transfer the cashews to a small bowl and cover with hot water from the kettle. Leave to soak for 20 minutes. Drain the cashews and add them to a food processor.

Peel the garlic and add the clove to the food processor along with the lemon juice, nutritional yeast, 130ml of cold water and a pinch of salt. Blend until smooth and combined, scraping down the sides as you go.

Transfer the cream cheese to a serving bowl.

Pick the leaves off the thyme and add half the leaves to the cream cheese. Stir until fully combined, then garnish the top with the remaining leaves, and serve.

Prep 10 mins, plus cooling   **Cook** 12–13 mins   £ £ £

DOUBLE BERRY CHIA JAM

We love the classy two-tone effect in this berry chia jam. As soon as you've made your way through the strawberry jam, the blackberry is ready and waiting. These jams are ideal for breakfast, whether they're lathered all over toast or spooned into a bowl of porridge.

Makes 1 jar

250g fresh strawberries
250g fresh blackberries
4 tbsp chia seeds
4 tbsp maple syrup
½ lemon

Rinse and pat dry the strawberries and blackberries, then trim the green tops off the strawberries and cut them in half.

Put the strawberries into one saucepan and the blackberries into another, and cook them separately over a medium heat for around 7–8 minutes, stirring frequently and using the back of a wooden spoon to break down the berries.

Reduce the heat to low and add 2 tablespoons of chia seeds, 2 tablespoons of maple syrup and half the juice from the lemon half into each saucepan. Cook for a further 5 minutes, stirring frequently, then remove from the heat.

Transfer the jams to a sterilised jar, pouring the blackberry jam in first so you end up with 2 distinct layers. Cover and seal the jar, then leave to cool completely. Store in the fridge for 2–3 weeks.

INDEX

(page numbers in *italic* refer to photographs)

ACKNOWLEDGEMENTS

When we started So Vegan three years ago, we never imagined that one day we would be the authors of a new vegan cookbook designed to change the way we all think about food. But here we are. *So Vegan in 5* has been an unforgettable journey and it is all possible thanks to everyone who has supported what we do and believed, like we do, in a future where people eat more plants.

First things first, we want to say a humongous thank you to our community. Without you guys, none of this would have been possible. Thank you to everyone who has recreated our recipes at home, shared them with friends and family, and sent in words of encouragement. We're super, super grateful and we really hope you love this book as much as we've enjoyed creating it for you.

Thank you to Ariella at United Agents for being a constant voice of reason from the start. A special thank you to Natalie at Bonnier for believing in us and giving us this opportunity to tell our story. To the entire team at Bonnier; Lisa, Clarissa, Ali, Kate, Francesca, Naomi and Oliver, thank you for all your hard work. And a big thank you to Carly for your patience and organisation. To Andrew, Lou, Lucy, Abi, Jo, Felicity, Rebecca, Julia and Evangeline, thank you for being amazing and for your help bringing our vision to light. We are so proud of this book and we couldn't have done it without any of you.

Over the past few years, we've been lucky to have so many friends and family who have helped us enormously along the way. We can't thank you enough for being there for us. Thank you to Joe 'The Videographer Extraordinaire', Ashley 'Mr Advice For Everything', Emily 'The PR Guru', Jake 'Photographer of the Year', Tim 'The Website Wizard', Marcel 'Shop Page Man', Toby 'El Bachelor', Ruth & Jason 'The Food Hoovers' and Sam & Emma 'The OGs'.

Thank you to So Vegan's number one fans, Ben's Dad and Roxy's Mum (we couldn't choose between you). To Beverley, Nigel, Pete, Anthea, Lucien and Liam, thank you for all the support and putting up with us talking about So Vegan all of the time.

Thank you to Paul for your wonderful support and to Suzanne and the entire team at Meat Free Monday for all your amazing work. To Sarah at Made in Hackney, Damien and Judy at Vevolution and everyone at Veganuary, thank you for everything you do for the movement. We're massively proud to be part of such a special community.

We received some amazing entries into our cookbook competition. Thank you to everyone who entered, and a massive congratulations to Laura and Claire whose recipes are totally delicious (you'll find them in this book!).

From Roxy, thank you to Chris for supporting *So Vegan in 5* and being a great boss. And from Ben, thank you to everyone at Mixcloud for not telling Xanthe, Nico or Nikhil that I was occasionally editing recipe videos at my desk when I was supposed to be working.

Lastly, thank you to everyone in the vegan community who paved the way for 'new vegans' like us to follow. Thanks to your passion and dedication, veganism has become one of the fastest-growing movements in the world and we're proud to be a part of it.

NUTRITIONAL INFO

	Energy (kcal)	Fat (g)	Sat Fat (g)	Carbs (g)
Almond milk (per 100ml)	67	4.5	0.5	4
Apricot & rosemary nut roast (per serving)	530	28	4	42
Artichoke & tapenade pasta (per serving)	652	25	6.5	79
Asian greens (per serving)	97	6	0.75	6
Asparagus tarts (per tart)	396	27	11	29
Baba ganoush (per pot)	255	21	3	5.5
Banana flapjack (per square)	188	6	2	28
Banoffee pots (per glass)	482	23	17	61
Beetroot, apple & coriander salad (per serving)	124	6	1	14
Beetroot hummus (per tbsp)	26	2	0.3	1
Berry cobbler (per serving)	446	10	1.5	78
Black bean mushrooms on noodles (per serving)	294	7.5	1	43
Black Forest energy balls (per ball)	197	12	3	16
Broccoli Alfredo (per serving)	650	23	4	72
Butter bean & artichoke dip (per pot)	905	75	11	33
Butternut squash hummus (per tbsp)	20	1	0.2	1.5
Butternut squash naan breads (per serving)	483	17	2.5	66.5
Cajun sweet potato fritters (per serving)	439	13	2	70
Cashew parmesan cheese (per jar)	553	35	7	24
Chickpea crisps (per serving)	219	9	1	20.5
Chipotle mayo (per tbsp)	23	2	0.2	0.2
Chipotle tomato rice (per serving)	250	4	0.5	46
Chive sour cream (per 50ml)	158	12	2.5	5
Chocolate & hazelnut overnight oats (per serving)	441	19	4	49
Chocolate & hazelnut spread (per tbsp)	83	6.5	1	4.5
Chocolate orange brandy mousse (per serving)	302	10.5	5	40
Cinnamon-roasted almonds (per 25g)	158	13	2.5	5
Claire's jam tarts (per tart)	311	15	6.5	38
Coconut banana bread (per slice)	277	9.1	7.5	43.9
Coconut chocolate bars (per bar)	333	24	19	23
Corn chowder (per serving)	276	13	2	28
Courgette tempura (per serving)	279	12	1	34
Creamy portobello mushrooms (per serving)	270	20.5	4	7.5

Sugars (g)	Fibre (g)	Protein (g)	Salt (g)	Sodium (mg)	Calcium (mg)	Iron (mg)
3.5	0.5	2	0.15	59	33	0.5
28	10	23	0.7	280	129	5.9
7	10	23	2.7	1095	267	2.2
5.5	3.25	3.25	0.85	341	119.5	2.15
4	4	8	1.18	473	46	0.8
4.5	8	6	0.5	209	153	4.4
10	3	4.5	0.09	35	25	1.25
51	5	5	0.3	71	34	1.3
14	2.5	1.5	1.3	552	21	0.7
0.5	0.5	0.7	0.05	19	11	0.27
31	6	9	0.8	212	178	1.1
5	2	13	1.5	604	31	1.2
15	2	6	0.11	43	47	1
8	14	33	0.6	230	78	4.5
4	20	16	1	421	52	4
0.5	0.5	0.6	0.04	14	12	0.22
10.5	8	12.5	2.8	1129	351	4.6
11	9	7	2.2	899	95	2.2
7	10	31	2.5	1017	27	4.5
0.7	7.5	10	1	400	66	2.3
0.1	0	1	0.18	71	0	0.15
8	3	6	0.3	121	17	0.7
2	1.5	6	0.5	201	19	1.7
13	9	13	0.65	262	47	2.2
4.5	0.7	1.5	0.02	9	13	0.4
36	3	8.5	0.5	204	57	1.8
4.5	0.5	5	0.17	70	58	0.73
22	2	4	0.44	177	54	0.8
26.4	1.8	3.9	0.3	100	90	1.09
22	3.5	3.5	0.1	39	12	1
4	4.5	8	1.5	603	11	1.24
2.5	3.5	6.5	0.94	376	143	1.9
2.5	3.5	12	0.75	109	27	2.8

	Energy (kcal)	Fat (g)	Sat Fat (g)	Carbs (g)
Creamy spinach ravioli (per serving)	746	41	7.5	69
Deep-pan pizza (per pizza)	1672	67	26	198
Double berry chia jam (per jar)	730	21	2	104
Easy peasy rice (per serving)	283	12	10	35
Fennel, rocket & orange salad (per serving)	197	7	1	24
Fluffy blueberry pancakes (*per serving)	471	13	2	76
Garlic & thyme cream cheese (per tbsp)	57	4.5	1	2
Garlic bread swirls (per swirl)	162	7.5	1.5	19
Ginger biscuits (per biscuit)	78	3	0.7	11.5
Gingerbread granola (per 50g)	235	8.5	1.5	32
Green pesto (per 100g)	646	45	5	24
Grilled cinnamon plums (per serving)	510	29	6	49
Grilled gem lettuce salad (per serving)	377	26	4	18
Harissa tofu scramble (per serving)	207	13	2	8
Harissa-roasted broccoli (*per serving)	267	21	3	5.5
Hoisin-glazed carrots (per serving)	125	4.5	0.7	17
Hoisin jackfruit bao buns (per bun)	287	8	4	47
Homemade ketchup (per jar)	279	0.6	0.1	54
Kale & sweet potato salad (per serving)	529	30	4.5	45
Key lime pie energy balls (per ball)	187	14	7	10
Laura's peanut butter & chocolate cookies (per cookie)	208	13	3.5	14.5
Lemon & coriander hummus (per tbsp)	41	3	0.5	1.5
Loaded sweet potatoes (per serving)	628	21	2.5	83
Mama's beetroot soup (*per serving)	262	8	1	37
Mango & peach sorbet (per serving)	148	5.5	5	21
Mango salsa (per bowl)	174	0.8	0.2	33
Minced mushroom tacos (per taco)	254	8	2	35
Mini passion fruit pavlova (per pavlova)	28	0.5	0.3	6
Mint choc chip ice cream (per serving)	440	32	25	34
Miso aubergine (per serving)	192	8	1.5	19
Mixed berry chia pudding (per serving)	375	15.5	5.5	43.5
Mushroom, sage & onion wellington (*per serving)	706	43	20	61
No-bake lemon cheesecake (per serving)	751	55	15	29
Oat milk (per 100ml)	89	3	0.5	12
Olive & rosemary focaccia (per serving)	303	7	1	51
Parsley & mint chickpea salad (per serving)	152	7.5	1	13
Pea & mint soup (per serving)	302	11	2.5	27

Sugars (g)	Fibre (g)	Protein (g)	Salt (g)	Sodium (mg)	Calcium (mg)	Iron (mg)
3.5	6.4	21.3	1.1	447	174	6.56
20	16	60	4.6	1857	948	8
73	43	13	0.07	26	199	3.3
1.5	4.5	7	0.33	132	54	1.5
22.5	9	5	1.3	516	147	1.6
28	5	9	1	404	276	2
0.5	0.5	2	0.04	16	4	0.6
0.5	1	4	0.57	228	35	0.7
5	0.5	0.8	0.16	65	27	0.43
14	3	6	0.1	25	46	2.5
7.5	11.5	32	2.56	1026	183	5.9
43	14	5	0.14	56	77	1.8
4	11	12	0.3	17	150	4.1
6	2.5	13	0.9	147	54	3
3	8	10	1.6	636	175	3.27
15.5	5	1.5	0.84	325	54	0.6
20	2.5	5	1.4	555	93	0.6
54	10	9	2.7	1092	117	3.75
19	15	12	1.2	496	324	6
8	3	4	0.14	55	11	1.4
9.5	2.5	7	0.24	94	20	0.84
0	0.8	1.5	0.19	76	23	0.45
17	20	16	0.9	266	197	8
13	7	7	0.6	1045	60	2.3
20	4.5	2	0.01	2	15	0.85
31	11	3.5	1	411	70	2.3
4	4	8	2.3	932	9	0.3
6	0.4	0.5	0	0	3	0
31	1.6	3.3	0.16	67.3	11.3	0.73
17.5	11	5	1.6	636	57	1.5
28	14.5	8	0.25	95	144	0
8.5	7	15	2.3	930	42	0.8
14	4	11	0.2	88.7	26.7	0.3
3.5	2	2.5	0.15	59	5	0.28
2	2.5	8.5	0.8	322	88	1.46
3.5	5	5.5	0.63	252	66	2.45
7.5	12.5	17	1.5	607	104	5

*Nutritional information is based on the lowest serving suggestion.

SO VEGAN IN 5

	Energy (kcal)	Fat (g)	Sat Fat (g)	Carbs (g)
Peanut butter & jelly breakfast slices (per slice)	272	15	5.5	25
Peanut butter slaw (per serving)	148	12.5	2	4
Peanut butter tofu zoodles (per serving)	527	43.5	7	17.5
Pear & chocolate cake (per serving)	346	13.5	11	50
Pulled BBQ mushroom burgers (per serving)	332	9	1.5	47
Purple linguine (per serving)	538	18	2.5	76
Ratatouille swirl (per serving)	158	8	1	14
Rich ragu (per serving)	670	12	3	92
Roast red pepper & walnut dip (per tbsp)	24	2	0.3	0.7
Roast tomato & basil soup (per serving)	209	12	2	19
Roast veg ciabatta sandwich (per serving)	341	16	1.5	36
Roasted Brussels sprouts (per serving)	118	7	1	7.5
Rosemary & thyme roast potatoes (*per serving)	344	7.5	1	60
Rustic tarte tatin (per serving)	276	13	5	36
Smashed peas on toast (per serving)	416	9.5	1.5	60
Smoky chargrilled corn (per serving)	154	11.5	2	8
Spiced pear porridge (per bowl)	396	9	1.5	61
Spicy gnocchi (per serving)	477	7	1	87
Spicy jalapeño guacamole (per pot)	367	35	7	6
Spicy sweet potato crisps (per serving)	295	13	2	37.5
Spinach & tofu filo pie (per serving)	459	25	3.5	31
Sticky Korean cauliflower bites (per serving)	183	1	0.3	34
Sun-dried tomato pesto (per 100g)	932	95	11	7.7
Super-green smoothie bowl (per bowl)	383	10.2	2.9	57
Super squash tray bake (per serving)	541	23	3.5	56
Sweet potato brownies (per square)	293	11	8	45
Tahini coffee shake (per shake)	761	47	17	58
Tangy potato & dill salad (per serving)	223	9	1.5	30
The carnival tofu burger (per serving)	559	16	2.5	80
Thyme & avocado bruschetta (per serving)	559	28	5	60
Tikka tofu skewers (per serving)	248	16	2	9
Toasted sesame noodle salad (per serving)	265	15	2.5	23.5
Warm Mediterranean couscous salad (per serving)	456	23	3	52
Whole-roasted cauliflower korma (*per serving)	404	30	20	21
Za'atar cauliflower steaks (per steak)	437	27	4	26
Za'atar wedges with tahini sauce (per serving)	288	15	2	29
Zesty lemon biscuits (per biscuit)	67	2	0.5	11.5

Sugars (g)	Fibre (g)	Protein (g)	Salt (g)	Sodium (mg)	Calcium (mg)	Iron (mg)
9	4.5	8	0.15	62	22	0.74
3	4	3	0.6	262	39	0.7
15	6	25	1.08	433	94	5
32	4.5	4.5	0.3	118	82	1.5
9	5.5	12	4.2	1703	91	1.3
6	6.5	14	1.3	528	60	2.39
13	6	5	0.76	304	36	1.1
11	13	32	1.97	788	50	3.2
0.6	0.4	0.5	0.06	26	4	0.19
16	6	4	1	824	63	1.54
8	7	9	1.4	552	29	1.2
6	6	3.5	0.27	110	38	1
3	6.5	7	1.25	498	23	1.1
21	2	3	0.23	91	37	0.49
6	9	18	1.5	402	192	2
2	2.5	4	0.26	102	18	1.8
23.5	9.5	13.5	0	0	320	1.45
10	8	12	1.5	598	147	4.5
3.5	8	3.5	0.2	69	32	0.8
10	8	4	1.38	551	81	3.9
4.5	8	25	1.8	727	133	2
15	4	7	1.8	728	53	1.4
3.5	1.8	11	3.96	1585	76	5.13
35.7	8.2	8.4	0.7	270	312	2
20	16.4	17.3	2.16	865	301	8.8
30	2.5	2.5	0.14	58	49	0.9
48	34	9	0.28	113	215	3
3.5	4	4	0.8	331	31	0.7
17	5	21	1.57	626	16	2.3
8	8	12.5	1.76	703	146	2
8	5	15	0.62	244	32	4.4
4.5	3.5	7.5	0.8	319	121	1.9
7	6	11	1.3	541	76	2.5
15	7	10	0.8	309	72	2.8
19.5	12.5	15.5	1.6	630	186	4
1.5	5.5	7.5	0.6	253	147	2.7
7	0.2	0.6	0.02	10	6	0.15

*Nutritional information is based on the lowest serving suggestion.

SO VEGAN IN 5

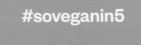
#soveganin5

Published by Lagom
An imprint of Bonnier Books UK
The Plaza,
535 Kings Road,
Chelsea Harbour,
London, SW10 0SZ
www.bonnierbooks.co.uk
Hardback ISBN: 9781788701235
eBook ISBN: 9781788701242

A CIP catalogue of this book is available from the British Library.

Designed by Studio Polka
Food stylist: Lou Kenney
Printed and bound by Estella, Spain

3 5 7 9 10 8 6 4

Every reasonable effort has been made to trace copyright holders of material reproduced in this book, but if any have been inadvertently overlooked the publishers would be glad to hear from them.

Lagom is an imprint of Bonnier Books UK

www.bonnierbooks.co.uk